THE ROMANCE OF HOCKEY'S HISTORY

THE ROMANCE
OF
HOCKEY'S HISTORY

M.K. Howells

Published by M.K. Howells
℅ The Hockey Association
The Stadium, Milton Kynes MK9 1NR

© Teddington Hockey Hockey Club.

ISBN. 0 950 1997 1 0

Printed by Ian Allan Printing Ltd.
Addlestone Surrey KT15 1HY
Telephone: 01932 855909

Content

Introduction 7

Chapter 1
Origins, Sport at Public Schools, Formation of Clubs 9

Chapter 2
Start of modern hockey, Characteristics, Duke of Clarence 15

Chapter 3
The start of Women`s hockey 39

Chapter 4
Revival of the Olympics, Team Games, GB withdraws,
the FIH 49

Chapter 5
GB returns, FIH acquire a world role 64

Chapter 6
The Appleyard Committee, the Future 76

Chapter 7
The Rules 81

Chapter 8
Umpiring 87

Chapter 9
The Stick 97

Chapter 10
The Hockey Ball 102

Chapter 11
Synthetic Surfaces and its introduction by a Joker 108

Chapter 12
Apochcryphal Tales of Hockey`s Antiquity 117

Appendices

1. Rules of the 1875 Association
2. Abolition of the bully
3. Team participation in the Olympics: some IOC decisions
4. Introduction of hockey to India
5. A world need for Synthetic Surfaces
6. Rugby and the Olympics
7. Conversion on the road to the Alchemists

Foreword

The author has been fortunate to have a wide experience of the game as a player and as several types of official including Committee membership of the International Hockey Federation.

He gratefully acknowledges a deal of help in confirming facts especially from overseas - and that includes the Research Department of the International Olympic Committee. A particular thank you is due to Michael Pearce, a one time President of the Richmond Club for his help with B.O.A., H.A. and English club records.

In covering a period of some hundred and fifty years there can be no cast iron guarantee of accuracy but with help from the above the facts have been carefully checked and are reasonably reliable. That does not necessarily apply to the author's opinions.

Introduction

The history of hockey is a romance no other sport can match.

There are absorbing claims of an ancient, illusory past. From a form of mimic warfare, the early game changed to one of gentlemanly, sporting behaviour supported by royal patronage, an advantage which helped it survive a difficult teething stage. It became one of the channels for the emancipation of women, who then demonstrated organisational skills much superior to those of the men.

The most popularly known characteristics of the rules - the bully and the circle - originated, fortuitously, from the qualities of sticks made of holly. Poor Indian street children were the indirect cause of the conversion of the game's `jolly hockey sticks' image to that of a highly respected competitive sport. The revolutionary, aggressive, non sports playing French of the late 19th century, changed their character and revived the Olympics. In their enthusiasm they illogically infiltrated team games, including hockey for which they set up a World Federation. One consequence was a take-over of the game's control from its British founders.

Generous conditions for hockey's Olympic participation stimulated the growth of national Associations. The machinations of a happy go lucky, Canadian, bachelor stockbroker brought about the introduction of synthetic surfaces to take the game into the 20th century; and just when the lack of spectator appeal threatened to impoverish the resources of its World Federation, the P.R. skills of the 1980 Olympic organisers, backed by sponsorship and instant world television, produced a large enough share of the resulting dividend to give the game a healthy financial base.

What more of a fairy story does one need?

Chapter 1

Origins, Sport at Public Schools, Formation of Clubs

How old is hockey? There are claims the game goes back to prehistoric times and was played in Egypt around 2000BC. Such claims do no harm. They convey an aura of antiquity. This is a book about the modern game so it was intended to leave it at that until it was realised that of recent years the theme has become a growth industry and someone, somewhere, ought gently to point to the odd inconsistency. It is not an easy task to do tactfully for if there is a fault it is only one of over enthusiasm. To maintain a sense of proportion some comments have been consigned to the end of the book.

The seeds of all stick and ball games played by one or two individuals were sown when man first rose on to his hind legs, picked up some sort of club and took a swipe at a loose object on the ground. Team activities were way into the future with hockey, give or take a decade or two, not beginning until around 1750. The quite distinct modern game, the one played today, started in the 1870's.

There has been no research, by the way, about the origin of the word `hockey' for regardless of the various claims (In 1870 Cowper described mud throwing by the boys of Olney as hockey) writers have used it as a convenience word applicable to any period of stick activity. For the French it has been an embarrassment since its pronunciation is the same as their word for hiccups. French ladies, when they started playing, felt it tended to debunk both their hoped for adventurous image and the undoubted attractiveness of their sporting ensemble.

Early living conditions

Life thousands of years ago was pretty basic - the survival of the fittest; living in closely knit tribes in wild country and meeting the next tribe only to pillage, rob or take their women. Travel, usually on foot, was hazardous. Communications were limited and there were no main roads. The expectation of life was less than 40 years.

Conditions many hundreds of years back were not all that better. Life expectancy had risen a little and in more advanced countries the tribes had been replaced by kingdoms with rulers and the ruled. There were four or five civilisations, e.g. the Chinese, Egyptians, Greeks and Romans, where the rulers served by their serfs were able to enjoy a degree of leisure. That did not mean having Saturday afternoon off for sport, although there would occasionally be annual, locally celebrated, festivals such as on midsummer day or at the end of the harvest. These might typically include contests of individual skills and strength such as jousting, wrestling, running, jumping, archery, discus and javelin throwing. There were no team games and the earliest known example of national occasions were the original Olympic Games from 776BC to 394AD, confined to Greece and able to be held only because of a sacred truce permitting safe conduct, during the period of the Games, to contestants who needed to travel through provinces and towns which in the normal course would be hostile to strangers.

Against such backgrounds one can understand more clearly that the likelihood of a particular pastime being played in one area some 4500 years ago and an identical enough one hundreds of years later in a different continent is remote and hardly proof of hockey's antiquity.

There were, undoubtedly, pastimes of one kind or another e.g. an 18th century Chilean activity of El Sueca or, more closely related, a festival game played by the Aztec Indians; but to claim them as hockey is stretching the imagination.

Aztecs at play.
Mixed hockey or a vanquished suitor?

Aztecs at play
Mixed hockey or a vanquished suitor?

The modern game

For the purposes of modern hockey there is little point in getting involved until about 1750 through to 1850. There is evidence over this period that forms of bandy, shinty and hurley - particularly the last in Ireland - were being played. The significance is not the frequency - nowhere near the level which some writers would have us believe - but the fact that a rough though recognisable pattern of play was beginning to evolve. To get a better understanding of developments one needs to look at sport in general, the start of regular games, the setting up of clubs and how the concept of sportsmanship arose. Consider first the political, social and economic background of that era.

The Napoleonic wars had left Britain deeply in debt. Until around 1800 there were really only two classes - the upper with all the wealth and the workers who lived in poverty and certainly had no time for games. They were employed for abnormally long hours in mines, factories and on the land working all day and into the night: and this included child labour.

The end of the wars around 1820 was followed by a recession and then, hesitatingly, a recovery. The British Empire was taking shape and stabilising. Exports trebled giving a period of commercial and manufacturing ascendancy over the rest of the family of nations, not from the efforts of the idle rich but from an emerging upper middle class. Understandably it led to political and social changes e.g. inroads into the parliamentary representation of the rotten boroughs, the Industrial Revolution, the passing of the Reform Act and the repeal of the Corn Laws.

Growth of public schools

In 1830 the first railway line was laid. By 1848 there were some 5000 miles of track. It widened the catchment area for Public Schools at a time of increasing demand brought about by the greater prosperity and growth of the professions as well as more frequent parental absence overseas for trading, exploring, colonial administration and service in the armed forces. A consequence was a rapid expansion in pupillage, with increases quoted for Marlborough from 200 to 500 over the 5 year period to 1848 and at Harrow from 80 to 438 over the years 1844 to 1859.

Hitherto, the academic masters of what were mostly smallish, sedentary centres of learning had taken little interest or responsibility for out of school activities, but, with this expansion, pupils became more and more undisciplined -trespassing, poaching, stone throwing and behaving generally well beyond the bounds of acceptability. The remedy with schools such as Uppingham, Marlborough, Harrow, Lancing and Loretto to the fore was to introduce compulsory games. Parallel with that Dr Arnold of Rugby had been a pioneer in teaching higher moral standards based on the view that pupils were in his care not just for academic purposes but also for character development. His example was followed at other schools, in particular by encouraging sport to be played for the game's sake. The story is fascinatingly described by Mangan's 'Athleticism in the Victorian and Edwardian Public Schools' (The Falmer Press).

Blue Coat hockey in 1880

Sportsmanship

With such developments the ethos of schools changed, revolving far less around the academic standards of learning and the scholarship of the pupils, more round the playing skills of the games masters, the sixth form athletes, goal scorers, run getters and team captains. The hero worshipping members of the lower forms looked forward eagerly to the days when they might be able to emulate their seniors who in turn were careful of their behaviour in order to preserve their images. It led to a new code of conduct called sportsmanship. One may not have thought about its origins but this is where it started, first to be carried forward to adulthood and then exported to the rest of the world. Without overlooking the lead given by the schools, it is a curious circumstance that credit for sportsmanship should rest with a group of children of an impressionable age who without control or example could as easily have turned to cruelty, bullying and viciousness.

The start of Clubs

Of more significance was that the boys so enjoyed the atmosphere and camaraderie of games that they wanted to go on playing after leaving school. By now adult cricket was becoming more common followed by a certain amount of soccer and rugby; but not enough for the growing demand.

A first move was to set up Old Boys clubs but few of them thrived. Members were still too widely scattered for the travelling conditions of the day. The next stage was for local clubs to be formed in the more prosperous residential areas where there were a sufficient number of like minded young men. Several of these clubs took root and games began to be played more frequently, first among the members themselves, then increasingly against neighbouring, so called, 'foreign' sides. It was a cardinal factor in getting sport off the ground. Until then leisure activities had been intermittent, unco-ordinated affairs but as the clubs multiplied and regular recreation became a habit, it led inevitably to the next step - the setting up of associations with agreed codes of rules.

Football, cricket and rugby took the lead. Hockey was some way behind for two reasons. First because fewer schools played; and of those which did, it was sometimes an Easter term option competing with athletics or even a continuation of the previous term's football. Secondly because each school seemed to have its own version depending upon the type of stick and ball, the size of the pitch and the surface e.g. the quadrangle, rubber ball and single handed sticks at Mill Hill or, as at Rossall, a sandy beach. School leavers wanting to join a club, had therefore to adapt and accept whatever variety was favoured; and because of this variety, a standard pattern was slow to evolve since foreign games, having to be preceded by a discussion on what rules were to apply, were seldom arranged.

The average game tended towards an unco-ordinated flailing of sticks. One can best portray the background by quoting from Cassell's 'Popular Educator' published in 1867.

`Hockey consists in driving a ball from one point to another by means of a hooked stick .....No simple rule is laid down as to the form this stick should take. It is simply a weapon with a bent knob or hook at the end, large or small, thick or thin, according to the option of the player, and used for the purpose of striking the ball, or catching it up on the point for a throw towards the goal. Hockey sticks, therefore, are of all shapes, sometimes in the form of a stout walking stick with a crook at the end.

The Hockey ball must be one fitted to receive hard and frequent blows. Anything in the nature of a cricket ball is found to be ill adapted for this peculiar game, as the leather soon bursts, through the effect of the knocks received from all kinds of rugged sticks. A large bung, strongly tied and quilted over with string, is a favourite and inexpensive ball for the purpose; and the best of all is perhaps a solid india rubber one, or the large part of a thick india rubber bottle, firmly closed at the end and from which the neck has been cut...

In commencing, the two parties meet midway between the goals, their left hands towards their opponents' goal and their right directed to their own. The ball is then thrown into the air by one of the party winning the toss. It may well be imagined that on the fall of the ball an exciting scene ensues. In an attempt to strike it, the hockey sticks are crossed in mimic warfare, and as it reaches the ground both sides surround it in a general scrimmage, while it is pushed, thrushed or struck by the hockey sticks, according to the chance which the various players may get of aiming at it. The hockey stick properly should never be raised much higher than the ground, for a dexterous shove at the ball may sometimes be quite as effective in serving the purpose of your side at a critical moment as a swinging blow, the opportunity for which may, indeed, very rarely occur. If the ball receives a good hit, and flies forward to the goal, a general rush is made in pursuit, one side aiming to follow up the advantage, and the other to overtake the ball first and restore the balance of the game. It will be apparent that in the rush and struggle of this description a fall or hard knock is exceedingly likely to occur, and Hockey is therefore not a game suited to weakly or timid players.'

The account continues with more detail and a few general rules but the above is sufficient to convey the general pattern of the game at that time. Why, then, against this background did hockey survive and eventually flourish? Quite simply, because there must have been an underlying feeling that here, somehow was a worthwhile game trying to find an identity - a potential combination of skill, eye, wrist, elusiveness and manoeuvre.

There was certainly a long way to go but at each stage of progress some fortunate feature occurred to maintain momentum. The first needs were reasonably level pitches and established clubs. Next a more easily controlled ball which would stay on the ground so that the rough, crude features of play could be replaced by more skilful manoeuvre and passing. It happened eventually but it had to evolve, sustained by a flow of recruits from the boarding schools.

Chapter 2

The start of modern hockey, help from the Duke of Clarence, developing its characteristics, the spread overseas

The Blackheath Club

First off the mark was Blackheath. They set up a Club in 1861 although they had played before that time. Their main sources of recruitment were the Old Boys of the local hockey playing Eliot Place Proprietary School. Their `Union` game was a variation of that described in Cassells Educator.

The start of a `Union' game

The ball was a 7 oz rubber cube, sticks were one handed, bound if preferred with wire. The teams normally consisted of 15 or more players and the pitch was approximately 200 yards long with goals 10 yards wide. A player could catch the ball and make a mark as in rugby. He would then retire four paces and take a hit either in the air or from the ground. A goal could be scored from any distance. Scrimmaging was the main characteristic and the cube obviously made passing or dribbling impracticable.

1871: The birth of the Teddington Club and modern hockey

In the 1860s Teddington was a village bounded on the river side by Hampton Court, the main entrance to which was along the beautiful chestnut drive of the Bushy Royal Park. A railway extension from London and the building of a bridge in 1863 resulted in the Teddington Cricket Club losing its ground. It was then fortunate enough to receive permission to play in the Park, through the intercession of Sir John Barton, Controller of the Royal Mint and deputy Ranger of the Park.

The members, having obtained permission to play, did not confine their activities to cricket and they began to look around for a winter activity. A few of them would have tried football, but it was not favoured in the district. Since stick games were becoming popular other members would almost certainly have tried out their paces in that direction.

Robert and John, the two sons of Barton, were active participants. Robert was the Secretary at the time. His younger brother succeeded him and later became the moving spirit and captain of an emerging hockey club.

A formal game did not immediately establish itself. However, 1871 was a poor summer and several inches of rain fell in the last four weeks of the season. One can picture the cricketers standing around discussing what to do and led by John Barton they decided to organise their hockey and have a proper winter club.

They had a mature membership playing for example married v single matches. They were not interested in the rough and tumble of hockey as it was then played. They knew the pattern of football with positional play, passing, dribbling and running off the ball: and it suited their numbers which were sufficient for two teams of up to eleven. So they fashioned a game on that basis, using their old cricket balls.

The use of a cricket ball was the crucial factor. A cube, bung or ring meant continuous scrimmaging, one handed play and an absence of passing, dribbling and individual skills. With the relatively level surface of the cricket outfield the free running cricket ball stayed more on the ground, a help in developing teamwork.

The suitability of some of the sticks was a problem, but there is no doubt that the adoption of the cricket ball, a limit to the number of players and a more level pitch were the catalysts which turned a free for all into an early form of the game which is played today.

Laying down the Rules.

But Teddington did more. Having hit upon an interesting new game they resolved to be methodical about its development. If problems of play arose during the game they were settled by the captains and then, if of general application, recorded as future rules. Teddington had about three years on their own to put an initial shape to their game, because, apart from Blackheath, no records or claims of other clubs exist before 1874.

Unfortunately an exercise book with records of the first three years was lost just before the last War. The rest of the records are in excellent condition and contain the minutes of rule changes which were made from time to time as described in more detail in Teddington's Centenary of Modern Hockey published in 1971.

Teddington had little or no wish to play anyone else nor had they thoughts of being pioneers of a new sport. All they sought was some form of exercise to keep them fit and in touch with each other during the winter months. It was a convenient choice because they had their old cricket balls, a reasonably level outfield in quiet, attractive surroundings and plenty of trees in the neighbourhood with which to experiment in making their sticks. Working out improvements to the rules as they went along e.g. the circle and the bully, was probably an added stimulus.

Enthusiasm of Richmond and Surbiton

Luckily, Richmond and Surbiton were nearby. Men of the Richmond Football Club in Old Deer Park had heard of the Teddington game and in 1874 decided they would like to try it as an offshoot of football. Teddington agreed to send some of their men over to explain the rules and get them off to a good start. Surbiton started in the same year and so in a small area beside the river Thames, hockey as it is now known began to get established. Richmond were progressive. They initiated matches with Teddington and Surbiton and sent accounts to the local press. The publicity attracted interest and by 1875 four more clubs, the Strollers, Upper Tooting, East Surrey and Sutton had been formed.

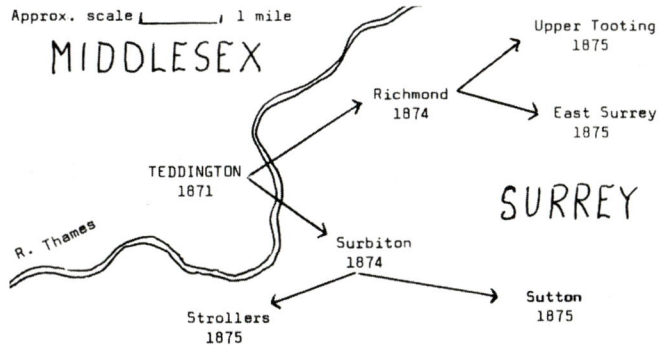

How the game spread prior to the formation of the first H.A in 1875.

Thus, as the diagram shows, there existed in close proximity a group of seven clubs all playing the same form of hockey. It was modern hockey's point of take off capped by a meeting called by Richmond to start a Hockey Association. It was important for another reason. Mr T.S. Haynes attended as a representative of the Blackheath Club and, as the press report records, stated that their game `was so totally different from the game played by the other clubs that he felt it would be perfectly useless for him to remain and give an opinion.'

Demise of the first Hockey Association.

Credit for the setting up of the first H.A. was due to the initiative and enthusiasm of Richmond strongly supported by Surbiton. Teddington, prefering to be insular, had agreed to an Association only after mixed views from their members and a decision on a majority vote. They did not, themselves, seek 'foreign' fixtures and to begin with seldom accepted more than two challenges a season - usually from Richmond and Surbiton.

The attitude was understandable. They had been playing on their own for a number of years and had worked out a settled code of rules to which they were accustomed. Playing someone else meant not only that half their members would be deprived of a game, matches had to be preceded by discussions about the application of the rules followed often by stoppages during play to explain their interpretation.

This first Association was premature and too local. With the inefficiency of the sticks and lack of support from its focal centre, enthusiasm waned. The four clubs formed in 1875 did not survive while for a few years both Richmond and Surbiton went into limbo. Teddington, as they continued slowly developing the rules, went on their independent way.

As it happened, a more compelling reason had arisen for their insularity - one which would later encourage growth at a stage when the game was in danger of going into decline or of disappearing altogether, for anyone making a forecast at that time would have backed hurley or the Union form of play as the most likely to become established.

Enter the Duke of Clarence

In those days Hampton with Teddington was what might be called Duke of Clarence country. The first Duke, later to become William IVth, held the historic appointment of Ranger of the royal Park of Bushy which carried with it free residence of Bushy House (now part of the adjacent National Physical Laboratory). A public house was named after him at Hampton Hill and there were two others at Teddington - the Clarence and the Adelaide which was named after Queen Adelaide, who succeeded to the appointment of Ranger when her husband died. There was also a Duke's Head.

The Duke with whom this story is concerned - and himself sometimes referred to as the Prince - was the eldest son of the Prince of Wales, later Edward VIIth. It is a fact that he learned to play hockey before going up to Trinity College, Cambridge and almost certainly at Teddington. There is no categorical proof, presumably because the occasions of his appearances and playing in the Park - relatively secluded in those days but nevertheless open to the public - needed to be kept confidential.

The circumstantial evidence is overwhelming. It goes like this.

1. John Barton, captain and secretary of the Hockey Club, lived in a grace and favour house in Bushy Park put at the disposal of his father, previously referred to in his role of deputy Ranger.

2. Barton was granted a commission in the Army and appointed ADC to the teenage Prince.

3. On the 30th October 1880 the Hockey Club held a special Committee meeting. Only four members attended, the President, the Captain and two senior members. The sole business was a proposal by the President seconded by the Captain that the following 'Gentleman' - W Trevenen Esq., The Palace, Hampton Court be elected a member. There is no record at the Palace of anyone with that actual name residing there at that time. It has been suggested that it was a nom de jeu - signifying three feathers.

4. There is then no evidence during the rest of the season of matches being played against other clubs and at a meeting in 1881 it was formally proposed and agreed that all such challenges be declined. However, at the same time, there was an unusual influx of nine new members who - speculating but see 6 below - could have been equerries, security personnel or even 'in the know' climbers on the bandwagon.

5. In 1883 the Duke went to Trinity College, Cambridge. They were asked if they would set up a hockey club for the benefit of the Prince, who, it was stated, enjoyed playing the game. It was coupled with a warning that 'he was wont to wield his club with more vigour than discretion.' (See Granta, Cambridge University library, 23.1.1892).

A club at Trinity was duly formed but a question with an obvious answer was - where had the Duke learned to play this newly emerging game known to be played at that time only in the Thames area just to the west of London? As the Prince's ADC, Barton, the Teddington Captain and Secretary, would hardly have taken him along to one of the few other clubs.

6. At their 1885 A.G.M., i,e, after the Duke had gone up to Trinity, Teddington agreed to resume playing foreign matches. The minutes of the meeting recorded the names of the members. Not one of the group which joined in 1881 appears in the list.

Footnotes

In 1991 the Government through the Secretary of State for the National

Heritage set up a Review Group of the Royal Parks. The report for Bushy Park stated, inter alia -

`Areas were granted for purposes other than parkland .. Cricket and hockey clubs were first given a helping hand.'

`Prince William, Duke of Clarence lived in Bushy House.'......

`A subsequent Duke of Clarence took to hockey which had been devised in the Park in 1871'

Miroy in his researches claims the Duke lived 'mainly' at Sandringham until in 1877, at age 12 or 13, he went to Dartmouth and then sometime in 1879 on a world trip in HMS Bacchante. Were this so he presumably had long holidays, particularly from Dartmouth, and there must have been a purpose in appointing as his ADC someone resident near Hampton Court and Bushy House.

DUKE OF CLARENCE: First President of the Hockey Association

JOHN BARTON ADC to the Duke of Clarence. First Captain and Secretary, Teddington H.C.

Suspended animation
Before following the Duke to Trinity step back and look at the overall situation.

Teddington after twelve years were firmly established but their independence made little contribution to the growth of the game. The folding up of the six other founder clubs of the 1875 Association - two admittedly temporarily - was a blow which left hockey at a low ebb. There were occasional reports of other clubs being in existence e.g. Mitcham, Forest Hill and two in Yorkshire, but few, if any, survived.

Of the several schools which continued to play in their Easter terms, the varieties of play were still more akin to the Union rules except for one bright exception. In 1876 Marlborough adopted the use of the cricket ball. Their game then grew in strength and some years later when hockey had established itself sufficiently at Oxford and Cambridge to justify having Varsity matches, it was their Old Boys who dominated the scene.

Class consciousness
Beyond hockey reflect upon the Country as a whole. The gap between the rich and the poor continued to be filled by members of the new professions, the colonisers, the entrepreneurs, the members of the Services and so on. Not surprisingly, there developed a social consciousness. Thackeray's descriptions in his classic Book of Snobs were gentle parodies of the attitudes of the so-called literary, aristocratic, military, clerical, university and other groups of that time as they contended for their place on this new social ladder. Status had become important for which reason the participation in hockey of the heir next but one to the throne was far more significant, and deserves more credit, than has been accorded in the past.

True then to the attitude of the day, when Trinity began its hockey the players were not a typical group of keen, enthusiastic undergraduates. Club membership was restricted to seniors and `carefully selected Dons'. Thereupon three other colleges -Clare, King`s and Caius - decided, in the hope of playing against the Duke, that they, too, would take up the game. Molesey was revived and a club was formed at Wimbledon. Both wrote to Trinity to arrange fixtures - although not, as far as can be ascertained to the other three colleges! And this, by the way, is not an occasion for a superior smile. As a measure of class attitudes it was typical of the day. The overall effect was to accelerate the introduction of hockey to the Universities and to give the game a general boost at a time of need.

Revival of the Hockey Association

Princely help went further for when in 1886 a second attempt was made to establish an Association, the Duke graciously agreed to be the first President. It was no mean accolade. Here was a modest new pastime starting off with royal patronage - a privilege certainly not accorded in those days to more popular sports such as cricket, soccer or rugby. Predictably it brought welcome publicity, maybe, with many a fond ambitious mother resolving her little Tommy would have to take up this fashionable new game. The royal interest was not temporary for as a schoolboy George V enjoyed playing the game. When Prince of Wales he too became President and, on his accession to the throne, Patron.

This second Association, the one which exists today, was set up through the initiative of Wimbledon who, playing on their Common, started with light sticks and string covered balls. One or two players, transferring from the hibernating Surbiton Club, soon introduced them to the cricket ball and the Teddington game. A year later a club was formed at Ealing. That was enough in 1886 to revive Surbiton.

Enthused by Wimbledon, representatives of these four clubs plus Trinity and Teddington met on the 18th January 1886 at the Holborn Restaurant in London to set up today's Hockey Association. Wimbledon and Molesey drafted the agreed constitution and code of rules and for a few years these two led the way in putting the Association on a firm, healthy basis: to do so was no simple matter but, after surmounting various hurdles, it was to be successfully accomplished. Sadly, the Duke died in 1892 but the momentum had started and by then two at least of the hurdles had been passed.

Notes:

1. As a College, Trinity had a lower ranking than a Club, but the invitation to become a founder member - not, one notices, extended to the three other Colleges - was one more example of a then class attitude which the others would quite naturally have understood and accepted.
2. Extract from Golden Jubilee Book of the Scottish H.A. published in 1951.

` The rapid spread of hockey is one of the minor marvels of the twentieth century. Before 1875 the game as we know it practically did not exist. Its name, on the other hand, is centuries old and its basic idea is almost as old as man himself ... There was an obvious need for the Hockey Association when it was formed by seven clubs in England in 1886. The game they standardised was one that met with prompt approval and it quickly spread. How inspired was the genius that so neatly satisfied what appears to be an almost universal appetite for such a game.'

Class Distinction

It was reflected in several ways. Officials wore top hats. Selectors would have their carriages, badges of rank and such adjuncts as shooting sticks. And - to quote - `Most players wear some sort of gloves. Old dancing gloves give ample protection; housemaid`s gloves with a little elastic I have heard recommended'.

Club colours were not red, blue or green etc. They were chosen with panache and enhanced sometimes with sashes.

Benson H.C.:	*Cerise and fawn cap, cerise sash*
Cambridge Univ:	*Cardinal and myrtle green*
Weston (Bath):	*White, chocolate and amber sash and cap*
Blundellsands:	*Olive green, maroon and salmon*

The four oldest surviving clubs, Teddington, Surbiton, Richmond and Wimbledon are probably unaware of their legacy of that period, for their colours of today still include such upmarket descriptions as chocolate, magenta, cherry and maroon.

The decorative cap evolved from public school cricket. Those worn by the 1st XI would be of a distinctive colour and awarded by the captain - hence the expression `being capped'. The House teams followed suit to produce a variety of colours to counter which the first team added a tassle. The idea was copied for county and international players.

According to the College of Heralds `Sash' came from the Arab "Shash" meaning a strip of muslin or ribbon. Its chivalrous origin developed from the leather shoulder strap used to support an Officer`s belt which carried his sword. It looked neat so was retained in material form for 'Dress` uniform and became a natural place for pinning on a medal. Next, should an Order be awarded, was to have a coloured ribbon as part of the award. The sash was born.

The modern game becomes established

Rise and fall of the Union game

The first hurdle was rivalry from the Blackheath game which had been copied by a number of other clubs. Stirred to action by the setting up of the H.A., their members countered by forming a Hockey Union having its main centre of activity in the Bristol area. For a while they were numerically stronger, but it was too late. Teddington since 1875 had continued quietly on its way refining the rules e.g. the circle, the corner, the corner hit stop, the bully and the introduction of umpire control. Then at an H.A. meeting in 1886 Slazengers introduced a prototype of a spliced stick. That meant the serious handicaps of the sting and the stick shape were on their way out.

It became more and more difficult for the Union to compete. In March 1895, it was dissolved `owing to the Association game gaining such favour and so many Union clubs resigning their membership and adopting the Association game.' Blackheath were doubly unfortunate for, in addition, permission to play on the Heath was withdrawn and for a few years they went into the wilderness. What must not be forgotten was that they were the first Club to put a form of hockey on the map and when they in turn revived and adopted the Association game their distinguished history continued.

The spliced stick

The introduction of the spliced stick at this stage, its rapid adoption and continuing refinement were cardinal factors in establishing hockey nationally. From Cassell's earlier description it began to change to a game of skill. Fresh ploys were used - the flick, the push, the jab, and lunge: books began to be written about tactics and the art of stickwork and manoeuvre. They also illustrated various strokes as shown on the next page. The rules were refined.

All round growth

Growth fostered by the Duke's participation continued. More clubs sprang up including sixteen in the North and independently enough to create their own Northern Counties Association with a request for group membership of the H.A. - willingly granted with a right to five delegates at H.A. meetings. Two ladies sides, Wimbledon and Ealing, were started.

Next, an accelerator rather than a hurdle. The game had spread to Wales while the hurley playing Irish decided to have a hockey playing splinter group. Wales, spurned initially by a much stronger England, challenged Ireland to an international match at Rhyl in 1895. England then changed their mind and offered to play the winner in London from which time the Home internationals became regular events. Later, when the Duke of York, the new President, supported by a large crowd attended an international at Richmond in 1900 that was one more seal of approval.

Some recommended strokes. The mainly horizontal arc of the hits show how easy it was to avoid giving the one time offence of `sticks' as opposed to the later Indian pattern which needed a more vertical arc.

First ever international match Wales v Ireland at Rhyl in 1895

Wales

Ireland

Survival

Having established itself the game had to survive and grow which, of course, it did, not only as a consequence of planned management but to a substantial extent through good fortune - the indirect effects of a conscious social status, both home and overseas, the growing struggle for women's emancipation and a relative absence of winter competition - soccer and rugby being the only rivals for men and lacrosse, perhaps, for women. There were, too, spin offs from Coubertin's revival of the Olympic Games, because the success of the French in getting hockey included in the programme encouraged countries in Europe to adopt the game and set up national Associations: and with India's subsequent successes becoming a stimulus for growth in Asia.

All these sources - yet to be dealt with - one might call physical factors.

Acquiring its characteristics

The above were only part of the equation. In the early years one or two unusual features were introduced. Not all have survived but they gave hockey its distinctive characteristics. The chain of events leading to their introduction was roughly as follows. With the clubs of the 1875 Association fading away after two or three years, there remained only a modest scattering of activity in the rest of the country until the involvement of the Duke of Clarence revived interest and led to the setting up of today's Hockey Association in 1886. While acknowledging phases of support from Richmond and Surbiton, it meant that Teddington had a fairly uninterrupted fifteen years to develop and think about the game. Had changes been subject to approval of other clubs or to a pooling of different ideas, the end result may well have been better; but progress would have been slower because the conditions and methods of play were still widely diverse.

At Bushy Park teams were chosen from the members as they arrived. Eight a side was enough to get started with latecomers then joining in. Winning, as always, was satisfying for the victors, but since the teams varied each week and thus had no corporate identity, it is easy - and necessary - to understand that enjoyment of the occasion continued to be more important than the result - enough to have an influence on rule making. Here are six examples. They are a far cry from the rule changes of today which need, perforce, to take account of their impact upon T.V., sponsoring, the spectators and such like.

1. The Roll-in

When the ball went over the side line the simple answer was to toss it straight back in, the players waiting for it to bounce before contending for it. That was extended to allow it also to be tossed towards the defending area. With more

The pitch in Bushy Park where the circle was first marked out is no longer used but its location was known. There can be only one such site and it is now permanently commemorated since on the occasion of the Hockey Association's centenary in 1986, and with the gracious permission of H.M. Queen Elizabeth, a chestnut tree was planted in the approximate area of one of the circles through the combined digging efforts of the Presidents of the International Hockey Federation, the Hockey Association and the Club - and with Surbiton representatives having an honoured place among the invited guests. In spite of the chestnut being a choice appropriate to the Park, on second thoughts it ought surely to have been a holly tree!

level pitches the toss was replaced by a roll-in along the ground in any direction, with the rest of the players behind a 5, later 7, yard line. As the game speeded up it became an increasingly pedestrian rule and was replaced by today's hit in.

2. Introduction of the Circle

In the pre spliced stick days, and in spite of the relatively level cricket outfield, hitting a hard cricket ball with a single piece of wood was not all that satisfactory. Different woods were tried e.g. oak, ash, hazel, maple and hickory. Then someone discovered that holly was whippy and produced longer hits - there was one account of the ball travelling 175 yards.

It was a mixed blessing. It spread the players out more but the aim of having a team game - of passing, dribbling, running down the wing and centering - began to be prejudiced. The culprit was one Teddington defender who started taking too many long, and often successful, shots at goal - successful because in those days there was no appointed goalkeeper, nor anyone wearing suitable pads; and although the ball could be stopped with the foot it could not be kicked.

To frustrate a tactic which the Club thought was spoiling the game - it was referred to as a `pernicious habit' - a decision was made first to limit shots at goal to those within a 15 yard line across the pitch and then to have a 15 (now 16) yard circle.

It was a logical decision at the time, but when goalkeepers, pads and kicking became the order of the day no-one seems to have thought of reviewing the rule. Eventually the circle became a permanent characteristic producing at each stage of the game`s advance inevitable complications for corner taking and circle infringements, not to mention the difficulties still experienced by ordinary spectators in understanding what the rule is all about. Today the circle remains a source of continuing revisions to the short corner rule but the consequences now of unravelling it, quite apart from the loss of a unique feature, would hardly justify the upheaval. The Rules chapter has further comments.

3. The corner rule

The introduction of the circle plus more efficient sticks led to a change in the corner rule. Until then the ball had been hit out from within a yard of the corner flag with no other players being allowed nearer than twenty yards. Now the defenders had to stay behind the goal line with the attackers outside the circle.

4. The ball stop.

From it followed another development, viz., stopping the ball from the hit out, which was adopted by agreement with Surbiton.

R. SLADE LUCAS

Joined Teddington as a schoolboy becoming successively Secretary, Treasurer and Club Captain. He was also a member of the H.A. Council from 1889 and later the Secretary.

A prolific scorer, a regular member for Middlesex and the South who would probably have played for England in 1895 had he not captained an M.C.C. touring side to the West Indies.

All secretarial reports and accounts prepared by Lucas were printed. Club fixture cards were retained, complete with results, to become a major part of Teddington`s early historical records.

It happened this way. Slade Lucas, one of the Teddington forwards was a renowned cricketer and hitter, and a well known member of the M.C.C. One day when he turned out against Surbiton their goalkeeper, the Reverend A.E.Beavan, refused point blank to play unless Lucas was made to stop the ball from the corner hit instead of taking a first time shot. The plea seemed reasonable enough in the circumstances, so the rule of stopping the ball was used by the two clubs and subsequently adopted generally. Perhaps goalkeepers might like to regard the Rev. Beavan as their patron saint!

5. The bully

Following the pattern of football, the first rules provided for the game to start with a simple hit off from the centre of the field and a 10 yard hit out, similar to the goal kick, when the ball went out of play over the goal line.

Between the 16th January and the 25th February 1875 (vide Teddington match accounts in the Field Magazine and the rules of the 1875 Hockey Association) - and at a time when the idea of the circle was being developed - a curious ritual, called a bully, was introduced both to start the game and as a replacement for the hit out.

As far as one can ascertain the expression 'bully' originated at schools as a general term meaning to contend for a ball e.g. the Eton Wall game starts with a bully and, whatever the particular variation, so did most of the early forms of school hockey. A hockey bully is rarely used these days - only to restart play after an unexpected stop. Here is a brief description. A player from either side faces his opposite number, with his goal to his right and the ball between them. Each taps the ground on his side of his goal and then the other's stick above the ball. The tapping above and to the side of the ball having been repeated three times, the two contend for the ball.

Why the unexpected adoption of such a ritual? The minutes, being formal, provide no evidence about the background but because the hit out, like the goal kick at soccer, was such a simple logical rule there just had to be a powerful reason. The more one studies the records and the timing, especially in association with the 15 yard line followed by the introduction of the circle, the more one has to conclude it was the holly stick.

The `pernicious habit' description implied not only that it needed to be discouraged, but that the hit out was regarded as too much of a penalty to the attacking side which had just succeeded in getting the ball as far as their opponent's goal -and especially so if one remembers that the shapes, bends and thicknesses of the home made single piece sticks meant their use for stopping was not wholly effective. To surmise, (Substantially confirmed by the background of its eventual replacement - see Appendix 2) it must have been agreed to introduce a rule which was less of a disadvantage to the attackers. Finding a suitable alternative could not have been easy: a one or two tap ritual may even have been tried first, but a third tap seems to have won the day.

So the introducer of the holly has a lot to answer for. He could never have foreseen its consequences. What strange impulse persuaded him to try the wood? Was he, perhaps, an arborealist who knew something? With its strong prickly leaves, it was not easy to cut and shape and not everyone adopted it. There were comments about supplies being scarce and complaints that some players were, therefore, using branches in excess of the then permitted two and a half inches circumference. If only the spliced sticks had been designed first! The tactical advantages they brought to the game with the push, scoop, flick and more reliable stopping would at that time have made repeated long hits seem rather purposeless. Today`s players may never have known about circles, short corners or bullies.

6. No Cups or Prizes

There was one more characteristic viz., the ban on leagues and games being played for cups or prizes. It came a little later -in 1892 - but it is mentioned here for completeness.

Matches were social occasions - for recreation between friends; and the fact that players might not be particularly fit or, by today's standards, their equipment and the playing surfaces were not all that efficient, was not important.

So when some keen enthusiasts suggested the introduction of leagues, it aroused a fear that the quality of the game and its carefully built up atmosphere of social enjoyment might be prejudiced. Wimbledon took the lead and in 1892 proposed that no club should take part in any hockey challenge cup or prize competitions. The other established clubs rallied round in support. Later, when the Rules Board was set up, Ireland asked for dispensation on the grounds that hockey in their country had to compete with other sports. These had cups and leagues and unless hockey did likewise they felt they would lose recruits. The plea was accepted and one has to admit it made little difference to international games except that the Irish umpires in those days were usually more alert.

Overall it was fashionable for this new activity of sport to be recreational rather than strongly competitive. Club cricket -except perhaps in the North - had no leagues and it was the heyday of such famous football teams as the Corinthians and the Casuals. Hockey seems to have been the only game in Britain which went to the length of actually banning leagues, cups or prizes; and when, inevitably, the outlook changed and overseas competitiveness increased, it was the obstinate retention of the rule which led to the decline in playing standards.

Becoming a world wide game

Once established hockey expanded rapidly. By 1900 England had around 200 clubs with the numbers continuing to rise each year. As with cricket and rugby it next spread overseas, mainly via the Forces, to the then Empire for reasons similar to those bringing about the start of sport in public schools viz, the soldiery had to be kept fit and occupied off duty - playing games provided a simple solution.

Colonials and members of the civil administration joined in. Facilities were readily available. Several well appointed, often residential, clubs had been built in countries such as India with local labour on hand to tend the sports pitches.

More modestly, and with the help of ex-patriots, clubs were set up in European countries such as Belgium, Denmark, France, Germany and Holland with national Associations being formed around the early 1920`s.

The game developed along three channels - the British men, the women and overseas men in that order of importance. Since the relative influence of the groups changed over the years the best way to paint the picture is to describe each separately until World War 11 and then, with control beginning to integrate, to concentrate on the game overall.

Benevolent Trustees

Most British players had learned their hockey under school conditions of virtual compulsory sportsmanship. Once the behavioural pattern had been instilled, bonuses accrued in terms of enjoyment as opposed to the pressure of competitive winning. When County matches were introduced in the 1880`s, the main object seemed to be to provide an excuse for those who could spare the time to have friendly mid-week games.

The administrative set up was something along these lines. The H.A. and, too, the Associations of Scotland and Wales were not dominant organisations. The work of the officials was voluntary. There were A.G.Ms., token affiliation fees to collect and national teams to be chosen from players paraded by the Divisional selectors. There was not much else. No tinkering with the rules. They had been agreed, so there was no need to alter them.

Everything revolved around the major clubs. Their views had influence. They were little concerned with a remote body like the Hockey Association. They just wanted to get on with the enjoyment of their game. Membership was a sort of closed shop. Fitting into the fraternity was more important than playing skills and once one joined one remained loyal. A player did not transfer to another club except from force of circumstances, such as relocation. He would probably not have been wanted anyway.

In the London area the fixtures were home and away, played to their best ability by members who in today's terms were not very fit. A club would never think of anything as remotely akin to professionalism as team training, which was why the young Oxford and Cambridge undergraduates, although less experienced, usually won most of their matches. There were no leagues to create a pressure to win. They were not needed. As long as it was a good game losing, within reason, was not important. One knew most of the opposition and played against them several times in a season. The peak occasions for enjoyment were the popular sociable Sunday games between teams calling themselves Tramps, Hornets, Bacchanalians, Ghosts etc. with players being members by invitation from the various Saturday clubs. Then there were the Wednesday county games and the Easter festivals. Very few players had cars. They travelled mostly by train and usually together for the more distant away matches when they would gossip or play cards. It all contributed to team spirit.

A different game.

What must also be realised is that because of the English type sticks, and often unsatisfactory grass pitches allied to winter weather, top hockey in those days was not a physical game of speed, stick skills, planned tactics and hard hitting. It was an exercise of different talents, more of intelligent movement off the ball into an open space - of timing and judgement in imparting the right speed to a flick or a push. Both were more effective than a straightforward hit of unpredictable pace, producing, probably, somewhere along its path an unexpected bounce, much more difficult to stop with the English stick than with one of Indian design. It was more thrust and counter-thrust.

Nor were players frustrated in their enjoyment and freedom of action by the negative attitude of man-to-man marking or the deliberate movement up field of a defender to put a forward offside. In reply to an isolated complaint about such a ploy the H.A. Secretary indicated that practices of that sort were not considered the done thing adding ` It is entirely against the spirit of the game; and if there are men who cannot play the game as it was intended to be played, they must be made the subject of severer legislation'.

To a similar questioning of such a tactic his response was:- `Do not criticise the rules. The rules were modelled for a game to be played by gentlemen as gentlemen.'

The general atmosphere, in other words, was one of a friendly contest, even with banter, against familiar opposition. There was no gamesmanship. A player would not question an umpire's decision except to own up if his infringement had been missed. It was not that they were impeccable sportsmen. Good behaviour was the accepted standard and even if instincts might occasionally be strained, there was no thought of stepping over the line. With pavilions being cold and utilitarian, the evenings would sometimes end with odd groups having dinner in the West End.

The Home Internationals

The highlights were the end of the season international matches. They were social occasions of modest pride, pleasure and status. The best way to appreciate the atmosphere is from the viewpoint of the officials who would be old friends. This included the umpires, chosen not because of their efficiency, more because of their popularity or service as ex-officials.

There were none of those fit, up and coming, keen interpreters of the rules who might want to take over the game, although there did, admittedly, come a time when the English began to make gentle noises about the quality of some of the other Country's appointments.

It was not so much the fixture itself: it was an occasion for a getting together of the establishment. They met and chatted the evening before. In the morning they would sight-see or play golf and this would include the players for it would not be considered necessary to have pre-match practice or training sessions. The result of the game was usually a foregone conclusion. But that did not matter. Goals were politely applauded: they were certainly not accompanied by gestures of triumph or national fervour. The occasion was looked upon as a display of the game at its best and an opportunity to honour the leading exponents with the award of an international cap.

A player representing his country would be expected to behave with a certain amount of dignified restraint. His kit would be clean, his hair brushed and parted. The shorts, of good quality serge, would reach to the knees and be well tailored. The international shirt badges were elaborate, e.g. the English rose of embroidered silk, the Welsh feathers of silver braid. There was none of this track suit nonsense. The team would stroll on to the pitch, usually with blazers and scarves, for a few desultory hits. On one occasion a keen, newly capped, player ran instead of ambled after the ball. He was advised by his captain not to tire himself out before the game. Senior English caps would not expect to stretch themselves at the outset and, since their colours were white, many would leave their sweaters on until they felt sufficiently warmed up. One well known Old Marlburian playing against Ireland - they had had the temerity to score first - received a fair degree of good humoured barracking when he waited until half time before finally disrobing.

Hospitality

The team and officials stayed at the best hotels. The highpoint was the formal dinner with dinner jackets or tails. The Scots and the Welsh had a particular relationship. In 1908 the Scots purloined - it was, of course, later paid for - a hotel silver rose bowl and filled it with port for all in turn to drink from at the end of the meal. The Welsh hosts had it inscribed with the result and took it to Scotland for the return fixture. The tradition arose that the visitors would be so well entertained that they could not be trusted to take it back safely. It was brought along the next year, duly inscribed, with the routine repeated thereafter. The bowl was mislaid during the last war and the tradition interrupted, perhaps in part because attitudes were getting keener, dinners less formal, or the matches were played as part of a tournament. It is likely other traditions existed. Questions at AGMs about the expense of entertainment at International matches from the body of the meeting were not unknown. The menu below, for example, has nine courses and seven wines - and that was only a Divisional dinner!

Post game refreshment

The favourite fixture was away to the Irish. Their hospitality was always a cut above the rest. Parties after the dinner would go on all night, followed on at least one occasion by a champagne breakfast. In Limerick in 1924 one or two of the players, took their partners to morning mass still in their (fancy dress) party clothes.

Typical of the predominantly social accent of the fixtures is an account in Dagg`s book on Irish hockey describing the arrival of their team at Liverpool in 1925, the day before a match against England at Birmingham. Since it happened to be Grand National day two of the players decided to stay on and go to the meeting. The financial results were disastrous. So one of them, who had acted successfully as a jester in his University troupe persuaded his companion to join him as a busker and give a variety show in the street - and with enough success to collect sufficient money to get to Birmingham just in time for the match.

In today's conditions on artificial surfaces it is probable that none of these International sides would have been fit enough to beat the 2nd XI of a National League club, but here in spirit and practice was a decade or two of hockey, if not at its best, then at its most socially enjoyable. It was certainly not the modern routine of playing ten or more internationals a year with sociability replaced by inquests on the results plus extra training sessions to remedy what had been regarded as defects.

An insular leaning

Although there was little attempt within the U.K. with their higher standard of play to spread the game abroad, it happened naturally via U.K. Forces overseas and enthusiastic expatriates or because it was becoming fashionable for countries, particularly in Europe, to take up one or other varieties of `le sport'.

During this period England would usually arrange one or possibly two European fixtures a year but the other Home Countries hardly any. The general approach might best, perhaps, be expressed by an extract from an article written in 1931 by S.H.Shoveller, a famous international in his day and a one time H.A. match and fixture secretary - "There is one branch of the work of the Hockey Association about which little is heard, namely - that which it undertakes as the parent body of the game. Its advice is often asked for and its decisions accepted by the hockey playing countries of Europe, by our Colonies of New South Wales, West Australia, New Zealand and South Africa and by India and Canada. The Hockey Association receives annually requests from various foreign countries to send over teams and whenever possible this is done for the furtherance of the game abroad." (Note: It was not very often and at that time only to Europe)

A decade or more later that really remained the extent of a passive attitude to the development of the game. The failure to realise the impact of the 1928 and 1936 Olympics not only upon India but also in Europe, particularly Holland and Germany, was a serious lapse. The growing status of the Games had become an incentive to train, to coach and develop a will to win. Social enjoyment, though ever welcome and present, was low in the order of priorities. With a widening during the war of the gap between themselves and their own players and a lack of F.I.H. contact, the H.A. began to live in a sporting dream world.

With the views of the players beginning to have more influence this becomes a suitable point for finishing with the early years of the men and switching to a similar period for the women, resuming the tale for both as part of the Olympic and FIH story.

Postscript:

A measure of the routine nature of the agenda at G.B. meetings was the amusement enjoyed by the rest of the Committee just after the War in listening to the inter-debate of the three national Secretaries. Socially they were close friends and colleagues but when it came to G.B. meetings some form of protective ego seemed to hamper their readiness to agree. The Welsh Secretary was of English origin, the English of Welsh. Each gave the impression he had a superior appreciation of the other Country's needs. The Welsh Secretary was also a lawyer; so, too, was the Scottish. Neither was going to cede a fine legal point to the other although both were willing to co-operate over any differences with the English. As a result discussions seemed to revolve too often around trivia. None of it really mattered because the agenda was modest, confined routinely to agreeing the dates and locations of future Home Countries' international fixtures, deciding whether or not there ought to be a Rules Board meeting solely on the grounds there had not been one for a long time; and reconfirming, since G.B. had opted out of the Olympics, that there was no call to accept one more request from the FIH for Board representation.

Chapter 3

The start of Women's Hockey

When women started playing they faced an uphill battle. Well beyond the middle ages muscle was more important than brain and they were regarded as the weaker sex in need of care and protection. Their place was in the home and their primary role was domesticity and the upbringing of children. They had beauty - a popular theme of poetic praise and admiration.

The Victorian era marked the peak of the phase and the start of its decline. As the class gap narrowed and the professions prospered, learning and intelligence took over from mere muscle. Women started to use more initiative and the campaign for emancipation began to take off. It followed national patterns although such factors as religion, e.g. Islam, also had an influence.

Class distinction had a greater impact upon women than on men. If, as suggested earlier, you read the Book of Snobs, have a go now at Pride and Prejudice, Barchester Towers or Vanity Fair remembering that the doctrine of sex discrimination had not even been thought of.

The leisured, gentler sex lived a sedate, conventional life. They did not work. They stayed at home to learn domestic skills -dressmaking, embroidery, piano playing, singing and household management - a preparation for marriage and motherhood with spinsters turning to such activities as caring for parents, charitable work, nursing or becoming governeses. It was this constraint on their mode of living which brought about the fight for emancipation. Taking up hockey, since it was a game for the middle to upper classes, was one opportunity of showing independence.

It was not an easy road. It encountered prejudice and obstacles. Consider clothing, finance, travel and obtaining a pitch. To lessen disapproval, one needed to be modest and discreet - a hat, secured with elaborate pins; a long sleeved blouse buttoned to the neck, a stiff linen collar, a tie and a voluminous serge skirt long enough to conceal the ankles. Travelling by oneself was frowned upon: one really needed a nearby team mate. Money could be a problem. Non-working ladies were not always financially independent, so parents had to be supportive. Getting a pitch meant finding an unprejudiced owner. Even then, although games were normally played midweek, the tenure might be cancelled at short notice if men wanted to take it over. The playing area also needed to be private, preferably with high fences `away from the prying eyes of young men'.

The popularity of the game increased but that did not allay concern for health. A doctor gave precautionary advice saying, inter alia, that although a men's team would change before and after a game and it was desirable for women to do likewise, it could safely be conceded that it was quite useless to expect eleven ladies to disrobe together in the same room: and although they would have to wear their normal underclothes, it would be as well for them to see if they could lessen the tightness of their stays, corsets and bodices, while realising it was also their duty not to prejudice their health by catching cold through the overheating of their body.

It was essential for them to don a warm sweater immediately after the game: that on the homeward journey each player should avoid the outsides of trams or buses and, if travelling by train, should try to secure a seat with one`s back to the engine. A warm bath on reaching home would probably counteract any chill which a strict observance of these measures had failed to avert.

Concern from another angle was expressed in the magazine `Hockey' by a writer as late as 1913. In his view, as long as woman remained in the sphere which nature intended, it enabled her to bring into play her many qualities including her glorious Being, her beneficial influence, her self-abnegation, her loyalty and affection, her supreme absence of reason, her lissome grace, her entrancing beauty of form and movement. (There was more but that`s enough). So the question was - is the playing of hockey by ladies beneficial to them in particular, to man in general and for future generations? Although one may concede under proper supervision that schoolgirls may play hockey, later on, `when the bursting bud has been woo`ed into the glorious peerless blossom', women with few exceptions should not do so. The strenuous nature of the game was likely to produce angularities, harden sinews, abnormally develop certain parts of the body, cause abrasions, even disfigurement. It would thus destroy the symmetry of mould and beauty of form, produce large feet and coarse hands. Fierce excitement would destroy the serene tranquil beauty of the features. The finest attributes of women - moral and mental and (its about time there was a minus) the constant lack of justice, or of honour, as inculcated among schoolboys under the general terms of being sportsmanlike, generally among women had very little scope, so leaving her peculiarly liable to display her weakest points in such a game.

The next edition of the magazine contained a dusty answer by a lady from Bowes Park H.C. who rated it as a lot of twaddle. Women played for fresh air and exercise, the love of the game and not least as evidence of the growing claims of women for their own independence of action. Women had chosen and these old ideas must go.

That in sum was the general drift: but the story has already moved too far ahead, so back to the beginnings.

A ladies club was formed at Molesey in 1887 followed shortly by others at Ealing and Wimbledon - very much the area of the first men's clubs. To start with they used string balls and light ash sticks. Oxford and Cambridge college sides were next and then one or two schools.

In 1894, a past and present Newnham College side arranged a tour to Dublin.

It must have been quite an adventure in those days for a group of young ladies; and not made any easier by snowy weather.

The Irish, having that year formed a Ladies Hockey Union, suggested the English should do likewise. After a return match at Brighton in 1895 where the subject was again considered, a Ladies Hockey Association was set up. An application for affiliation was made to the Hockey Association, who politely declined on the grounds that their's was a body solely for men.

Royal Holloway College team – 1888
The College were founder members of the AEWHA

The ladies harboured a certain amount of resentment but the men were not so much unchivalrous as cowardly. There was still plenty of emancipatory disapproval around and, being conscious of their royal patronage, they did not want to get involved. They also disapproved of mixed games and clubs.

So the ladies went their own way - and maybe to lessen the gentler sex image - decided in the title of their Association to change the name from `Ladies' to

'Women'. Not everyone agreed and a number of the County Associations and clubs remained 'Ladies'. By 1898 there were 52 affiliated clubs. A newspaper offer of a challenge cup was declined and members were reminded that none of them should play for cups or prizes. Around that time a Welsh Association was formed with Scotland following in 1900.

Growth overseas

Meanwhile clubs, though not yet Associations, began to appear overseas - first in Canada and the U.S.A., then five or six years later in New Zealand, Australia, Rhodesia, and South Africa. The Europeans, apart from Denmark, and Holland who played a two sided stick game of their own, were late starters. For them emancipation was a slower process.

In spite of this widening spread, the rate of progress was slow, for suitably level pitches were not easy to find and there were still pockets of disapproval around. One bright exception was the ready adoption of the game by most fee paying girl schools.

More remarkable, was its introduction to America in 1901 by an Englishwoman, one Constance Appleby, who, starting at Harvard, became for many years Director of Physical Education at Bryn Mawr College. As interest in the game grew, she obtained help from England by encouraging coaches to go over during the summer vacations to assist at training camps. She lived to an age of 107 and after her death a commemorative window was dedicated to her at St John's Church near her birthplace at Burley in the New Forest. Her enthusiasm, and the sporting principles she inculcated, made hockey for women one of the most popular sports in the United States.

They in turn reciprocated with considerable support for the International Federation of Womens Hockey Associations, always attending Conferences and tournaments and hosting two of their own, one at Philadelphia in 1936 and another at Towson in Maryland in 1963. During the War they clubbed together to provide the U.K. with three ambulances.

Their growth in the early years had another impact - a lessening of the few remaining pockets of prejudice against the women's game in the U.K., the real take off for which came after the end of the first War. Their valuable work in the factories, on the land, in offices, hospitals and as Service auxiliaries quite changed their stature, image and self assurance, helped, fortuitously, by an emerging fashion of postcards which, as illustrated, had a generally glamourising effect.

While the men continued to build up the exclusivity of their clubs, the women now concentrated on developing their game. Clubs, Counties and Divisions were revived and new ones were formed. The AEWHA recruited, trained and then graded umpires. They also set up coaching courses and circulated training films.

A CHANGE IN ATTITUDE

FROM DISAPPROVAL TO APPROVAL

AND EVEN TO BANTER

A boost to esprit de corps occurred during county and other trial games by adopting a practice of social performances. It started with representative groups being required to sing or put on some sort of act or display. The practice became a feature of women's hockey throughout the world. The extract below from the menu of the 40th anniversary dinner of the AEWHA in 1935 is a typical example.

All England Women's Hockey Association.

1895   1935

Friday, March 1st, 1935.

The President, **MISS H. M. LIGHT**, in the Chair.

Programme.

SPEECHES by PAST PRESIDENTS:

MOCK TRIAL.
    East Anglian and Southern Counties W.H.A.

PIERROTS.
    Western Counties W.H.A.

THE BIG FIVE, or
    How the Public got the true Story.
    Midland Counties W.H.A.

PAGEANT of the COUNTIES.

A typical pre-war dinner programme

To some degree it was an answer to the early days of the men who because of limited club accommodation would repair after a game to a room at the local hostelry. With a pipe being a symbol of manhood, many occasions developed into so called smoking concerts when, with at least one member able to play the piano, there would be community singing of favourites like Molly Malone, Old Father Thames and Annie Laurie. Such forms of relaxation could not be for women. They were not expected to frequent public houses.

With the results of trials and tournaments being regarded more seriously, self entertainment among women`s teams has disappointingly become less frequent. Even so, as recently as the Inter-Nations Cup at Padua in 1988, an umpire`s first international appointment was still marked by the rest of her colleagues with an elaborate baptismal ceremony, the victim being led into a room by an escort of white bed sheeted attendants and presented to the senior official robed as a high priestess. The neophyte, having been commanded to kneel and bow her head, was then baptised from a chalice of gin and tonic or suchlike and solemnly dubbed with her future `tournament' nickname.

To revert - by 1930 the A.E.W.H.A. were claiming 1200 clubs rising to 2100 in 1939, roughly double the number for men. Then there were the schools encouraged by their P.E. mistresses many of whom played in the national or divisional sides. Their school support and enthusiasm produced outstanding numbers of spectators at international matches leading to the use of the Oval in 1935 and, when that became too small, to Wembley with a claimed peak in 1976 of 68,000. It became the Mecca of the women`s game with overseas sides competing for invitations to play there even after the introduction of artificial surfaces.

Women`s hockey in those years was enormously buoyant, especially compared with the men who, because of their different approach, could rarely muster gates above 5000.

The I.F.W.H.A

International tours came next. There had in fact been a truncated trip to Australia and New Zealand in 1914, the players managing to get back just before the start of the War. In 1921 a visit to the U.S.A. gave thought to the setting up of a World Federation. The concept met none of the reluctance that had been shown by the G.B. men and a firm decision to do so was made in 1924 during a return trip by a U.S. team: but it took until January 1927 before the Federation was founded, the first members being the four Home Countries, Australia, South Africa, the U.S.A. and Denmark. The `Objects', successfully achieved, spoke volumes - `To further the best interests of the game among women of all nations and to promote friendly intercourse among the players'. Nothing about `control' or having championships. A disappointment was that the F.I.H. discouraged their emerging women's sections from joining.

In 1936 the United States hosted the IFWHA Conference and tournament at Philadelphia. In addition arrangements were made for the visiting teams, separately or in pairs, to tour most of that Country's hockey playing areas - one with a brief overlap into Canada - for exhibition games or matches against local opposition. Accommodation was usually provided individually in the homes of their hosts thus, in accordance with the Federation's objectives, `promoting friendly intercourse' and sufficiently so for many of the players in the U.K. to find themselves the recipients of food parcels during the War.

Conference tours then became the standard practice. They were planned with imagination, enthusiasm and efficiency. In 1950, the South Africans really used their initiative, hiring a train in Cape Town for a three month tour from Salisbury in Rhodesia and back to Cape Town with 27 stops, some sightseeing but mostly to spread the message of hockey with exhibition games or, if preferred, matches against representative local groups - and all with plenty of sociability.

The visiting teams were not necessarily their countries' best players: not everyone could spare the time or cost. If a country could not provide a full team some players might still travel and join others similarly placed to form a mixed side: and since, whatever the make-up in those early days, the skills of the English would be head and shoulders above the rest, the question of competitive nationalism or playing to find a tournament winner never arose. The object was to encourage the spread of the game by giving demonstrations at their best and most enjoyable. Everyone had a grand time. As for the subsequent tour matches over wide areas, their attraction to large numbers of spectators, the general sociability and the mixing of the players, must all have contributed, however modest the degree, to the amity of nations.

As the hockey sections for women in the European Associations grew stronger they looked forward to joining in the tours but, clumsily, in 1939 the F.I.H., apprehensive about the growing popularity of the IFWHA, refused to allow their members to join. They were then out on a limb. Unlike their men, they had no Olympic hockey to look forward to and now were not permitted to join in these attractive world trips with the I.F.W. At the end of 1948 the FIH sensibly changed their minds whereupon Belgium, Austria, Switzerland, Holland, Germany and France all applied for membership.

Meanwhile the Conferences, tournaments and tours went on -Folkestone, Sydney, Amsterdam, Towson in the U.S.A., Leverkusen (Germany), Auckland, Edinburgh, Vancouver and finally Kuala Lumpur - each a prime example of efficiency, management and enthusiasm, the succeeding tour ever seeking ways to improve upon the one before. It is doubtful if any section of sport has ever done so much , and so successfully, to promote the image and growth of its game, quite apart from the healthy boost it must have given in various areas of the world to the development of womens' independence and self management.

But all good things must come to an end and that was to be the fate of the I.F.W.H.A. details of which must wait until the reader has been given the story of hockey`s introduction to the Olympic Games and the formation of the International Hockey Federation.

The IFWHA flag designed by members of the Scottish W.H.A

**Evidence of enthusiasm.
Car numberplate of Grace Robertson, when President of USAFHA**

BARON PIERRE DE COUBERTIN
An idealist. Founder of the modern Olympic Games.

Chapter 3
Revival of the Olympics, Infiltration of Team Games, GB Withdrawal, FIH and India help establish Hockey as an Olympic Sport

The Olympics

By the turn of the century the Olympic Games had been revived. For the first thirty odd years they had no material influence on hockey: but the eventual consequences were highly important - for the world spread of the game, because of the gradual take-over of control from the British founders, and, indirectly, for the introduction of artificial surfaces and the achievement of reasonable financial stability by the then Governing Body.

Such consequences justify what may next appear to be an over concentration on what at the time was a minor aspect of hockey's history, a time when one would have thought the centre stage would have been taken up by accounts of widespread growth within the U.K., in the then Empire and by women's hockey.

Enter Coubertin

The seeds of British sport had been spreading. A German, Guts-Muts, suggested a revival of the Olympics, then Zappas. a Greek, made an unsuccesful attempt to do so in 1870. Brookes, an Englishman, had earlier created his own local Olympic Association at Much Wenlock in 1850: though modest in extent, the games there still take place.

More dedicated was Baron Coubertin, a French aristocrat, who spent his fortune studying and pursuing the development of sportsmanship.

To learn more he visited England - including Much Wenlock - where he was particularly impressed by the public school philosophies of muscular Christianity and a healthy mind in a healthy body. He also visited the U.S.A. where the Universities had taken up sport. In 1892 he presented proposals at the Sorbonne for a revival of the Olympic Games.

France was not a sporting nation at that time and such activities were banned at the Sorbonne because it was thought they would interfere with studies. The immediate response was not, therefore, particularly encouraging with one or two of their newspapers claiming it was simply an attempt to copy the British.

If, as originally in Greece, the proposals had been confined to the one country, they would admittedly have had scant chance of success. But

Coubertin was pursuing something much broader - an international event as described in his oft quoted words "Let us export our oarsmen, our runners, our fencers, into other lands. That is the true Free Trade of the future; and the day it is introduced into Europe the cause of Peace will have received a new and strong ally."

He persisted with his campaign and two years later organised another Congress, also at the Sorbonne, attended by sports representatives from twelve countries. There it was agreed eventually to set up an Olympic Committee with its headquarters in Paris and Coubertin as Secretary General. The revival of the Games was earmarked for 1896 - Athens, appropriately, having the honour of being the first host city.

Thirteen nations competed in nine sports such as athletics, fencing, swimming, archery and weightlifting. Observing the tradition, all were contests between male individuals - no team games and no women.

Those were the bald facts. To appreciate the breadth, the imagination and the ambitious nature of what had been contemplated, one needs a reminder of the background.

The 19th century was not one to look back upon with nostalgia. For France it had been a particularly bitter period, having begun during the last days of their Revolution under the shadow of the guillotine. Then came the disturbing impact of Robespierre, the debilitating Napoleonic wars, including the long Peninsular campaign, Egypt and the battle of the Nile, the retreat from Moscow, Trafalgar and Waterloo. There was an attempt to restore the monarchy and two more Revolutions before a Republic was finally established in 1870. There were non-stop successions of alliances and counter alliances usually about boundary disputes, and mostly associated with military action, for or against Belgium, Holland, Austria, Italy, Luxembourg and spreading as far as Hungary, Rumania, Poland and Turkey. The period ended with the defeat of the French in the Franco-Prussian war. There was much suffering, poverty, and civil unrest. A partial lessening of pressure during the last ten years came from a reversion to Empire building mostly in Africa and Asia, but that still meant having to compete against other European 'builders`.

With such a backcloth one might expect that international sport would have been about the last activity to occupy the minds of the Europeans. That the French should, nevertheless, want to undertake an Olympic revival seemed almost as if they were seeking a mission to help put these unhappy years behind them.

Europe was certainly in need of some form of moral stimulus but in pursuit of such a change of philosophy, the work of reviving the Games, the selling of the idea, the organisation and administration must have been formidable tasks. Communications - internationally, the railway system was in its infancy - were poor: long distant telephones were few and unreliable. The average country would have no particular affection for its neighbour or a visiting foreign spectator: accommodation would not be readily available; and international contests involving physical contact were hardly likely to be social occasions as within Channel-insulated Britain where opposing Home Country groups of athletes might well include a colleague or two from the same school or university.

In spite of these and, doubtless, many other problems, the French led Committee persevered and succeeded at last in getting the project off the ground.

The Paris Olympics

To maintain the momentum of Athens, Paris agreed to be host city for the 1900 Games, tackling the job with energy and enthusiasm, attracting a further nine nations and four times as many competitors. The organising committee decided it should be, first and foremost, a festival of sport. A World Fair was held at the same time leading to confusion - especially it was said to Coubertin, now the I.O.C. President - about who was running what.

For their own participants a Union des Societes Francaises de Sports Athletiques (USFSA) was formed with sub-committees for the various activities. New events were introduced - croquet, golf and, significantly, the team sports of cricket, polo, football and rugby. There was even an attempt to include hockey, for one or two Paris clubs did exist. The English were not interested. Theirs was the only country where the game was played regularly, and neither a Scottish Association, nor a Rules Board to provide a common code of play, had yet been set up.

Apart from team sports not being a feature of the original Olympics, attempts to introduce them, other than casually as part of the World Fair, were over ambitious. The various British Associations had no objection to individual players taking part, but because sport from the schools upwards was well established, the then superior level of British play was such that full international contests would have amounted to non events.

To the players, competitiveness and national identity were unimportant. Cricket well illustrated the casual nature of the programme. A Devon County Wanderers side with two Americans on their strength had decided they would visit Paris. A twelve a side match was arranged with a local team, La Belle France - expatriates with just one French national. The Olympic results ever after record a British win of a gold medal against the Union des Societes Francaises de Sports Athletiques although doubt is cast about whether a medal was actually issued or whether the Wanderers, who were just joining in the general celebrations, knew the occasion was to rank as an Olympic event. It was cricket`s only Olympic appearance but it created the precedent of a team game. As a classic example of the rippling effect of a stone tossed into a pool, one has only to reflect upon the widespread consequences of hockey`s subsequent inclusion.

If cricket`s participation was token, rugby`s first inclusion might be described as opportunist for the Rugby Union refused to be involved and the English

Olympic Awards

When the Games were revived at Athens in 1896, each winner, as originally, was crowned with a garland of olive leaves collected from the area nearest to the one time sacred grove at Altis.

Records of what happened at Paris in 1900 are vague. Not all contests were Olympic events and olive leaves from Greece were unaccessible. There were loose references to medals, gold awards and even to laurel wreaths.

Gold medals had undoubtedly become the vogue by the time of the 1908 Games in London and they were more practical as mementoes.

It is not certain when the practice of silver and bronze medals was introduced. They were not awarded for hockey in 1908 -although the Scots were given commemorative medallions - but that could have been because those who would have qualified came from the other Countries of G.B. in the name of which England had already won the gold.

The cost of hockey`s first medal was £2, i.e. the equivalent of two gold sovereigns, paid for by the British Olympic Committee.

The rugby consisted of a game between a touring Wallabies side and county champions Cornwall.

Since the Rugby Union would give no official recognition to the event, the B.O.C. decided they could not award medals. They did, however, present inscribed certificates to the winning Australian players.

players were left to please themselves. As a consequence and with the summer over players from the Birmingham area, having finished their various Saturday games, formed themselves into a team, travelled to Paris overnight, played and lost to a French side, got on their figurative bicycles and arrived back home in time for work on Monday morning. (Three subsequent `appearances' and the interesting circumstances of rugby`s Olympic fade-out are described in Appendix 6)

St Louis, 1904

The New World was offered the 3rd Games. Too far away for most Europeans, it attracted only half as many participants as at Paris and half as many sports. Maybe as a fill in, the innovation of team events was copied with two entries - lacrosse (it appeared again in 1908 and then dropped out) and football.

London and the inclusion of hockey

The 1908 Games were awarded to Rome. When they subsequently withdrew, London agreed to take over. Then at an Olympic Congress at the Hague in 1907 without any request from the H.A. who had, admittedly failed to accept numerous invitations from the British Olympic Committee to attend their meetings, hockey was put in the programme. From what evidence there is, the initiative came from the Union des Societes Francaises de Sport Athletiques and there is a Hockey Council minute agreeing to the British Olympic Committee accepting a French hockey application. The French in turn persuaded Germany to participate in the guise of a team from the Uhlenhorster Club. Prospects for a worthwhile tournament did not seem all that bright.

Officially the U.K. entry had to be Great Britain but in order to make it more of a tournament it was agreed that England, Scotland, Ireland and Wales should enter separate teams with the winner (England) then being recognised as the official G.B. representative. It was also assumed - as happened - that since two of the other three Home Countries would be second and third, there should be no official second or third placings.

In addition to the hockey, there was some football and rugby, all of which took place in October long after the competitors for the normal Games, contested in August, had gone home. In keeping with the traditions of the day, it had been accepted automaticlly that such events should not be allowed to interfere with the cricket season. Such fixtures were sacrosanct.

More control

Coubertin was an idealist rather than an organiser and the fairly happy go lucky approach, of which the above was an example, needed to be controlled. An

I.O.C. meeting at Luxemburg in 1910 suggested there should in future be a properly defined programme. The idea was pursued at the next meeting during the Stockholm Olympics in 1912 where, since it was not a game Sweden played, there was no hockey.

Rather than continue with 'Une grande latitude' the Committee after reflecting upon the fundamental principles of the Games decided to split the events into three separate categories described as 'indispensibles, desirables et admissibles'. The first, and major, category would apply to all the traditional contests between individuals such as wrestling and athletics. The second would relate to modern sports such as cycling, skating, yachting, lawn tennis and, notably, because it gave recognition to team sports, rugby, football and hockey. The third group was defined as 'other sports of an international character, played by at least six countries' and which a host country would be permitted to introduce for the occasion subject to a minimum level of support. The second and third groups were soon after amalgamated into an optional 'facultatif' category. The minimum number of countries was increased from time to time but the proviso that inclusion rested with the host country was retained.

Meantime in that same year at Hamburg there was a meeting of hockey playing countries at which England proposed the setting up of a European Federation. It foundered over the inevitable obstacle - a condition that there should be no leagues or games for cups or prizes.

Antwerp

Because of the War there were, of course, no Games in 1916. The I.O.C. had a brief meeting after the Armistice, chose Antwerp as the host city for 1920 and decided also to use the occasion as an opportunity for a full Committee Session and a general review. Let us first deal with the hockey angle.

The bitter fighting, in which Belgium had suffered more than most, had not long finished. Here was an opportunity for sport to help get life back to normal. It was a little soon for the losers to participate but support was expected from others. Belgium was one of the pioneers of European hockey, so encouraged by France what could be more natural for its other close allies, England (representing Britain) and Denmark, to have a tournament. Again it was played separately after the main Olympics had finished.

The English could not have found it very satisfying. They beat Belgium 10-1 and Denmark 6-1. France, having already lost to Denmark 9-1, gave them a walk-over by failing to turn up after indulging too much the night before at a sumptuous dinner to which they had invited the English with the intention, it was unkindly suggested, of putting them under the table.

The experience seems to have crystallised the minds of the British for they then resolved to participate no longer in an event for which they had had little enthusiasm. Such tournaments did not conform to the creed they imposed upon their clubs of not playing for cups or prizes: and, being so much stronger, they were embarrassed about the risk of being accused of `pot hunting', a term of disparagement very common in those days of amateur idealism and sport for sport's sake.

(The attitude had long existed. It might best be described by an extract from The Cricketer Magazine which reporting in 1906 on the A.G.M. of the H.A. commented -
` There is no desire that hockey should become a spectator game. There is enough pleasure in it without artificial excitement being engendered by competition. Pot hunting in any pastime is an ignoble pursuit and hockey administrators have made up their minds there shall be none of it in the game with which they are identified')

The 19th I.O.C. Session

From a broader angle the Antwerp meeting was a landmark in the history of the Olympics.

Pre-war, the Games, fuelled by Coubertin's idealism and French enthusiasm, had in a way been on trial. They had certainly gained in popularity, but if the occasions were to become firmly established they needed to be better organised with proper guidelines and a standard programme. The haphazard inclusion of team sports was one example of an indecisive I.O.C. approach with a rough 50/50 split about whether or not to accept them. There was by coincidence an early item on the 1920 agenda recommending the exclusion of all team sports except football. But whatever the decision, in the absence of proper guidelines and depending upon the venue, it could well, later, be reversed.

The most important feature of the Session was a paper `The Constitution and Laws governing modern Olympism' presented by Count Baillet-Latour, a Belgian pramatist and an efficient organiser who would later succeed Coubertin as the I.O.C. President.

It included a code of rules for the future running of the games plus proposals that every participating country should have its own national Olympic Committee and each sport its World Federation to act as co-ordinators and channels of communication with the I.O.C. There would then be regularly held Olympic Congresses, attended by representatives of the two bodies, at which any recommendations they might wish to make could be considered.

The proposals were agreed and began straight away to be implemented. It meant that while hockey had no World Federation, it could no longer participate. Moreover, in the light of the 1920 recommendation to exclude team games, even if a World Federation were subsequently set up, that would not of itself guarantee I.O.C. acceptance of hockey as a participating sport.

COUNT BAILLET-LATOUR
Successor to Coubertin who set up National Olympic Committees and
World Federations for each participating sport

From the British point of view they must have felt that would now settle the matter for, quite apart from the team games question, the one sided nature of the two hockey occasions which had been held held so far, hardly merited the description of `tournaments'.

Admittedly, a case might have been made by then for a further attempt to set up of some sort of international body because, in spite of its modest depth, the game was spreading: and from 1922 there are H.A. minutes referring to applications for affiliation from such Commonwealth countries as Victoria (BC), Colombo (Sri Lanka), Australia, Kenya, South Africa and Jamaica. But were the H.A. to organise something - they were the obvious body - it would almost certainly exclude the Olympics and be on their terms in respect of cups or prizes.

In the event the British took no action. The French persevered and wrote to the H.A. pressing for the setting up of a Federation. The H.A. prevaricated. A second request followed and at a Council meeting in July 1922 it was resolved after a brief discussion, that the subject should stand on the file until the next meeting. Three months later - the last item on the agenda -it was again held over. In March 1923, on the assumption they would have to take the lead, it was resolved 'The H.A. could not undertake such a large proposition'. The French, meanwhile, had, hopefully, made an application to the Paris organising committee for the inclusion of hockey in the 1924 Olympics. It was refused because there was no Federation. There was another nail for hockey`s seeming demise. Rugby and polo*, the two remaining team games apart from football, had decided 1924 should mark their last appearance.

The French were not going to give up for two reasons - both emotive rather than logical. Against the sombre background of the 19th century they had successfully launched a revival of the Olympics. However minor its part in the programme, they were not, therefore, going to agree to the withdrawal of one of the events, even a team game, without a struggle. The other reason was that such a struggle would now be led by a Federation Francaise de Hockey. The Union des Societes Francaises de Sports Athletiques had earlier agreed to cede responsibility for French hockey to this newly established body, the Committee of which were clearly determined that one of their earliest duties was not going to be attendance at the funeral rites of the game`s Olympic participation.

Encouraged by their President, Paul Leautey, they decided to take matters into their own hands. They canvassed and obtained the support of six other European Associations - Belgium, Austria, Hungary, Czechoslovakia, Spain and Switzerland - and on the 7th January 1924 set up a Federation Internationale de Hockey with Paris as the registered headquarters.

* Polo appeared unexpectedly in Berlin in 1936 but then vanished from the Olympic scene.

PAUL LEAUTEY
President: Federation Francaise de Hockey
First President: International Hockey Federation

The British were then invited to join but did not accept. They would have had an awareness through the B.O.C. of the strength of the Olympic wish to eliminate team sports; and with their far greater numbers and hence their superior skills, there must at that period have appeared little point in supporting the idea of Olympic hockey.

For the Federation the next step was to obtain I.O.C. recognition. Europe was the centre of Olympic activities and, superficially, seven countries may have appeared a fair continental representation. On the other hand the British were not among them, it was their game and they controlled the rules. Furthermore, the I.O.C. had only to take account of playing strengths and they would have seen a much different picture.

Player distribution

For example, a measure of the difference may be gauged from some readily available statistics. There is a record as far back as season 1913/14 of the H.A. having over 500 affiliated clubs together with their numerous hockey playing schools while in 1922 the women`s A.E.W.H.A. had just under 1000 clubs plus their schools. To these must be added the players in Scotland, Ireland and Wales. Next there were the affiliates of most of the ex 'Empire' countries who at that time, with the exception of India and the Armed Forces, generally observed the no cups or prizes principle.

By comparison those European Associations which formed the F.I.H. (The Dutch were still playing their own type of game) had very few clubs - probably less than forty in total and amounting to under 2% of the then hockey playing community.

Even so the I.O.C. appeared to have no hesitation in recognising them as bona fide world representatives of the game and at their 23rd Session in Paris reinstated hockey as an Olympic sport in the `facultatif', i.e. optional, category. It is difficult to understand what motivations and interests were at play. The British, whatever they thought, did not interfere or protest. The I.O.C., because of its President, the make up of the Committee and the Paris location may have had a French leaning. But they they must also have had a left hand and right hand state of mind for, having recommended the exclusion of all team sports, apart from the special case of football, they had thereupon not only accepted another team game, they had done so on the application of a body not representative of the sport as a whole.

Importance of French initiative

However confused the circumstances, in making a judgement in the light of today, there can only be respect, even praise, for the initiative of the French. But there should also be understanding for the attitude of the British. The mostly English hierarchy were not just fuddy duddies. Over the years they had transformed a one time potentially dangerous stick game of `mimic warfare' into a popular, civilised pastime played to a jealously guarded degree of sportsmanship which they were anxious to preserve with participation and enjoyment being more important than winning.

It was not the end of the matter. Whether or not team games should be included in the Olympics remained a continuing source of debate. Some examples, with the accent on hockey, are shown in Appendix 3. A following appendix offers reasons why the French did not follow suit with rugby in spite of it being for them a much more popular game.

Ever since, in spite of a modest playing status, France has maintained its leading role in the F.I.H. The first three Presidents were French, so was the Treasurer who officiated for 34 years and, of course, there is the current President who before his appointment had held the office of Secretary from 1966 till 1984. There was another stalwart - from Switzerland - Albert Demaurex. He actually spent his playing days in Paris with the French Racing Club but his was a remarkable record - Secretary from 1929 to 1950 and Treasurer from 1958 to 1981.

Hockey re-enters the Olympics

After the events of 1924, i.e. hockey's Olympic exclusion followed by the setting up of the F.I.H. and its formal I.O.C. recognition, there was no option but to allow the game's inclusion in the 1928 programme at Amsterdam should that be the wish of the host country. It was. The Dutch changed over from their own form of play to the conventional pattern, affiliated first to the F.I.H., next to its National Olympic Committee and then applied for inclusion. Germany also entered and - the first non European country - so did India. By 1928 F.I.H. membership had risen from 7 to 14. Some of the Associations might have been regarded as lightweights. These three recruits had muscle and became the medal winners.

The Dutch won the silver medal and in doing so attracted large crowds and plenty of gate money. A greater stimulus, which drew world attention, was the winning of the gold medal by India, the impact of which has still to be described.

To the I.O.C. both hockey and the F.I.H. had, overnight, acquired higher profiles, the significance of which will be clearer by returning for a moment to the broader I.O.C. picture.

In 1925 Coubertin, after more than thirty years in office, had retired as President. He was succeeded by Baron Latour who, being aware of the importance of keeping the Games up to date, added as a standard item of the Congress agenda a regular review of the programme. Inevitably, discussions led to differences of opinion, to pressure groups and how to get a quart into a pint pot.

To begin with there had been no women. Coubertin had been strongly opposed to them because they were barred from the original Games. Then no team sports or demonstration sports. Then demonstration sports were a good thing: fewer events per sport was the answer, or fewer optional sports or an updated selection and so on. The rising demand for optional sports was met by stricter qualifying conditions including the requirement of being played in at least 6 countries, raised successively to 10, 20, 25, 40 or more and, today, with a minimum of 3 continents.

With its widening world spread hockey managed to keep ahead of these limits; but there was the other condition - that, since it had to bear the cost, the inclusion of any optional sport was subject to the agreement of the host country. That was the rub because hockey's acceptance had tended to be marginal and between 1896 and 1928 it had only participated twice.

As with all team games it required more players and therefore more accommodation. A tournament was time consuming. A 100 metres race, seldom with more than one competitor per nation, attracted a large crowd and was over in seconds to make way for the next event and keep interest alive. A game to decide the winner of two hockey sides would take an hour and a half and be just one of a series of pool games followed by semi finals and a final.

Until 1928 matches had not attracted many spectators. With grass pitches of variable quality, many games were scrappy; and not only were the rules difficult for the ordinary spectator to understand, traditional good behaviour led to few outward signs of partisanship and a consequent absence of atmosphere. With no T.V. or sponsorship in those days, it meant a hockey tournament was usually run at a loss.

So the F.I.H. continued to be apprehensive when, as emancipation progressed, the I.O.C. eased their attitude to the general participation of women and decided that their modest five to six events should be brought nearer to the men`s sixteen or seventeen. How would they be fitted in? Would some men`s events have to be pared down or excluded? And Demonstration sports? Some had more spectator appeal than hockey and had begun to infiltrate into the programme. In spite of the boost at Amsterdam hockey was not home and dry, especially as it was known at the time that the 1932 Games would be hosted by Los Angeles.

The Los Angeles Games

The American men did not play hockey so, as in the case of the St Louis Olympics in 1904, it was not expected to be included in the programme. That would mean a break of at least eight years before another opportunity arose - a long time for an isolated team game competing in a crowded programme against the claims of newcomers.

Fortunately a series of unexpected events occurred. A month or two after Amsterdam, recently married Henry Greer, whose wife had been an enthusiatic English hockey player, arranged a men`s match in Philadelphia. Other games followed. Although few and localised, they were enough for him to decide in 1930 to set up a men`s Field Hockey Association of America. That did not mean Olympic hockey for, even were the group to be accepted as representatives of their country, there seemed little prospect of any opposition. In those pre-air travel days, with the time and cost that would have to be spent on a long sea journey, it was unlikely any European country would want to join in what, quite apart from the impact of the looming Great Depression, would be a low key tournament. With subsidies from benefactors, as happened in 1928, India might be willing to participate, but two teams would hardly constitute an Olympic tournament.

Nevertheless, in 1931, i.e, with just a year to go, the American Hockey Association - by then they had six clubs - went through the necessary formalities of affiliating both to the F.I.H. and to their own national Olympic Committee. Shortly afterwards the U.S.Olympic Committee, presumably encouraged by the F.I.H., put hockey in the programme. India applied to participate whereupon Japan, having in turn first affiliated, did likewise.

(An Irish padre had introduced hockey to Keio University in 1905. A report states it continued to be fostered there for 16 years before any clubs were established, although a team of mostly British expatriates gave them occasional games. A Japanese Hockey Union was formed in 1923. In spite of their lack of experience they were enthusiastic and must, at least, have fancied their chances against the Americans.)

The results were not very exciting. India beat Japan 11-1 and the U.S.A. 24-1. Japan beat the U.S. 9-2. As a spectacle the tournament was a P.R. disaster with the 125,000 seats of a new Olympic stadium looking a little empty.

The consequences

In spite of the experience, the F.I.H. must have breathed a sigh of relief. They had at least managed to maintain a continuity of Olympic participation. What neither they nor the I.O.C. realised - or so this book contends - was that as long as team games continued to be admissible, hockey would now have the option of being one of them.

India, although an undeveloped country, had recently come into the world limelight through Ghandhi`s policy of civil disobedience and fasting, followed by his political campaign for national independence. With poor countries, such lights tend to fade, but not for one which at Amsterdam had won an Olympic gold medal, an honour then virtually exclusive to the rich, mainly European, nations. Every country needs something of which to be proud and India`s national pride at their success had been unbounded. The rest of Asia and parts of Africa bathed in the reflected glory.

Another gold at Los Angeles had confirmed their quality with a convincing win in a tense Berlin final against Germany four years later re-inforcing it. Had the I.O.C., for whatever logical reason, sought now to exclude hockey from the programme there would have been a public outcry based on accusations of jealousy and bias against an underprivileged country which during its struggle for independence had just demonstrated an area of clear superiority.

The outlook

With a virtual guarantee for hockey as an Olympic sport this might be an appropriate moment to review the state of the game.

By now it was represented by three distinct groups - first the British men, leading exponents and guardians of the rules, secondly the bouyant International Federation of Women`s Hockey Associations; and thirdly the FIH, to start with all Europeans, not highly skilled or numerous, but the required channel for participation in the Olympics.

Each had a different outlook. It is difficult to find an analogy. The nearest one can think of is to picture an attractive woodland area planted by the British men who were sitting back, content with their labours and happy for others to come along and enjoy the atmosphere as long as they did nothing to spoil it. The new entrants, the women, were full of enthusiasm, finding the prospect so attractive that they began to enlarge it by planting lots more trees and arbours. The FIH also found it attractive, but their more opportunist approach was to start building a protective fence around it, so constructed that the only way in would be through their entrance.

All were facing an unknown future - one which would bring about remarkable changes to the rate of growth, to the balance of influence, to the equipment and the efficiency of the game. It is not easy to maintain a sense of perspective in describing the effects of such factors. The best starting point might be a reminder of the British attitude with discernible elements of elderly parenthood, reluctant to give its children more freedom; yet in performance terms still way ahead of other countries except, possibly, India.

Chapter 5

British Hockey returns to the Olympics, FIH acquire world role

But that was a view taken without knowledge of a pending World War. It would be twelve years before the Olympics were revived. Given the pre-knowledge, what sort of forecast would have been made of hockey's future?

Much would depend upon the stumbling block of playing for cups and prizes, a natural enough progression which the European members of the F.I.H. had wished to introduce too soon - before the standard of their play merited such aspirations - and which the British, steeped deeply in the past, had resisted for too long.

It looked, admittedly, given continuing Olympic participation, as if the keenness and enthusiasm of the French would bear fruit. But the British were not just obstinate. They had borne hockey's birth pangs and survived its growing pains. The French had not. Would the new era modify the British outlook, produce new blood and a more forward looking attitude for a future which was by no means straightforward?

For example, a sizeable section of the I.O.C. had remained opposed to team games. India, having secured its independence, would be less in the public eye and maybe weaker, especially as it had been compelled, not wholly harmoniously, to hive off a considerable area of its country to form the new State of Pakistan. In spite of the publicity and euphoria from two of the past three Olympics, hockey had still only participated five times during the forty years of its revival; and, except for world popular football, there were now no other team games.

The I.O.C. were more remote having transferred their headquarters from Paris to Lausanne. In 1942 they had suffered the loss of their experienced President, Comte Bailleur-Latour, who was succeeded by Sigfrid Edstrom from non hockey playing Sweden. As for the F.I.H. they were, perforce, less active because Georg Evers, their President from 1936 until 1945, hailed from Germany.

Add to this a reminder of the overall position. Hockey was a game designed wholly by the British. They controlled the rules and, counting their women, still had more clubs, probably, than the rest of the world put together. If other countries or clubs wished to take up the game, they were free to do so; but that did not mean, ipso facto, having an automatic say in rule making or control. It would take time and a fair amount of growth for that to happen.

Combining these outlooks and angles - especially the twelve year gap caused by the War - one possibility might have been to see the game reverting to a predominantly Commonwealth sport with Olympic participation being replaced by normal rounds of international matches between neighbouring countries;

and with G.B., either as a result of outside pressure or from its own initiative, agreeing at last to accept responsibility for setting up a wider world body including the absorption or demise of the F.I.H. The likelihood would be stronger if hockey happened not to be included in the first post war Olympics.

Such a prospect could not have been more wrong. Not only was London nominated as the next host city, the British reaction led unwittingly, to the occasion becoming a stepping stone from which, after some twenty odd years, the necessary centralised control would at last be achieved - but via the F.I.H.

There were several factors. In case the thread gets lost among the detail, here are the headings of the separate strands.

1. A British reluctance to break free from pre-war traditions, their declining track record in the field, their lack of interest in taking control and the importance of the club.
2. Generous qualifying conditions for hockey`s Olympic participation with a consequential increase both in F.I.H. affiliations and status.
3. A stable period of quiet F.I.H. consolidation under the Presidency of Quarles van Ufford of Holland assisted by Rene Frank of Belgium as Secretary.
4. The introduction of the Indian stick and its three consequences - higher stick skills, greater competitiveness and a need for rule revisions.
5. The effect of increased competitiveness within the International Federation of Women`s Hockey Associations.

The post war scene. F.I.H. progress towards world control

For British hockey, the I.O.C`s early preparations for the resumption of the Games in 1948, were, presumably of passing interest since they would not, of course, be involved. But -plans of mice and men - in the absence of volunteers London was prevailed upon to be the host city. And then, the unexpected, hockey was included in the programme.

The British heirarchy still had no wish to join in, but there was pressure from above viz,. it was the duty of all sports to make the Games a success. It was an important post-war celebration signifying the return to peace. Britain was the leading hockey country, it had invented the game, it was one at which they excelled and they were the host country. Not to participate would be churlish. There was no option but to join in. To quote from an unenthusiastic H.A. minute "The Council considered that it was advisable for a team to take part". Few other words could have conveyed their feelings so appropriately and succinctly.

To the F.I.H. the choice of London was a stroke of luck. They had been formed for the purpose of Olympic hockey. That was their raison d`etre - no Olympic hockey, no F.I.H. Now after the twelve year gap, not only had Olympic participation been confirmed,the forced inclusion of G.B. meant the founders of the game had to come to them, almost cap in hand, and apply for affiliation.

The dilemma

In applying to join the F.I.H. the British had two options - to pay lip service to the requirement, treat the occasion as a one-off exercise and then revert to isolation. The other was to be realistic - to accept the changing postwar attitudes and not only join for the future but use the opportunity to merge the F.I.H. and the Rules Board into one body with the reasonable expectation of having a degree of executive influence. Were any fears about sporting standards to be realised, they could then be resolved from within. More importantly, if they were to compete in the Olympics again, this was likely to be Britain's last opportunity to join with any degree of muscle.

A wrong decision

The Home Countries chose the first option, having resolved privately that if there were hockey at Helsinki in 1952 - and it was by no means certain for at that time Finland played only ice hockey - they would not participate. As a consequence, instead of joining separately as fully pledged member Associations, they merely `adhered' as a G.B. group. Nevertheless, they had to accede to a quid pro quo - token F.I.H. representation on the Rules Board.

With hindsight - always an easy source of judgement - it was the wrong decision; and what made it worse was that when in the event Finland took up field hockey and had it included at Helsinki, it immediately became clear that the only option was to take part. The British fraternity - and the players with their silver medals - had so enjoyed the experience of the 1948 Games that, as soon as it was quietly mooted they would not be joining in, the instant indignation from the few who learned about it was so strong, the thought had to be stillborn. That meant, as the F.I.H. continued year by year to grow in membership and influence, a weakened hand in resisting their pressure for greater representation on the Rules Board.

There has to be sympathy for the efforts of the G.B. officials to do what they thought best. Their's was simply a different perspective, made more distant by the War years. The Europeans, having been through harder times, having suffered severer political, social and physical upheavals, were a little shorter on sporting ideals.

Nevertheless, although their game had been more firmly entrenched and their playing strength greater, the British had never sought to lead the Europeans. Now, even had they wished to, the scope for initiative had gone, for not only had the choice of London consolidated hockey's future participation in the Olympics, it had stimulated a big increase in F.I.H. membership. By 1948 the number had risen to 23. At Helsinki it had become 31: and membership went on rising because of another quite unexpected factor.

Five Ring Fever

The Olympic Games were attracting more and more world interest. An athlete would sacrifice a great deal to achieve the honour and prestige of representing his country and in general the competition to do so was fierce. With popular events such as sprinting or free style swimming there would only be one or, at the most, two national places available.

For hockey in the early days the scope and opportunities were easier. Sixteen national sides were allowed to compete with each team squad consisting of eighteen players: and they were not necessarily the sixteen best teams for the choice involved a geographical spread to permit each continent to have representation.

In several countries the game was a minority sport, maybe with under a dozen clubs. That was no problem. The drill was simple. They just had to form themselves into a national Association, affiliate for a modest fee to a welcoming F.I.H. and then join their national Olympic Committee. The final step, through the F.I.H. was to apply to take part.

As an awareness of the opportunities grew, there were even cases of athletes from other sports transferring their allegiance e.g. as a goalkeeper or a speedy winger. In the U.S.A. this keenness to change to hockey in the hope of making the national side and becoming an `Olympian' was popularly referred to as Five Ring Fever.

The consequential rise in the number of national Associations, compared, for example, with those of the more commonly played non-Olympic sports such as cricket and rugby, increased both the apparent status of the F.I.H. in the eyes of the I.O.C. and its authority in demanding from the British greater representation on the Rules Board. For the British, of course, it meant a corresponding decline in their standing. (See graph overleaf)

From 1973 as the competition from other sports to participate in the Olympics increased, the I.O.C. reduced the number of eligible men`s hockey teams to twelve and the squad numbers to sixteen. By then, with Olympic participation virtually automatic, and women about to be included, the F.I.H. were in sight of achieving full control of the game.

The Indian Stick

The period happened to coincide with another milestone - the introduction of the Indian stick. No-one at the time could have conceived its revolutionary impact: and it was unfortunate for the British that the change occurred during a period when events were moving against them.

The interesting circumstances of the Indian stick`s adoption are described in the Sticks chapter. Its early appearance arose from expediency - a scarcity of exports from England plus reduced manufactures during World War 11. The

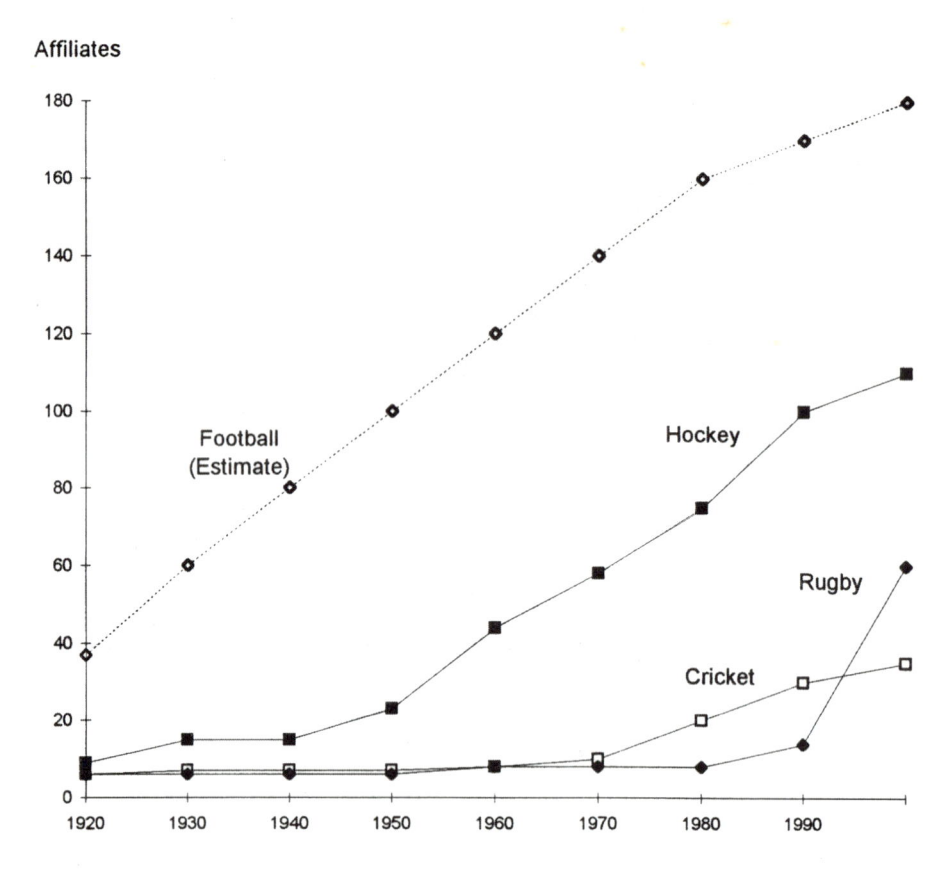

**Examples of affiliations to World representative bodies.
Period 1920 to 1990**

Notes:

1. Hockey's take off started after the 1948 London Olympics partly as a consequence of "Five Ring Fever".
2. In the early years the representative strength of the F.I.H. flattered its status for it did not control the rules and operated only for the four yearly Olympics. A number of its affiliated national Associations consisted of less than 20 clubs.
3. Later when the FIH acquired rule control and extended its activities to tournaments other than the Olympics, its authority became total.
4. Appendix 6 has comments about rugby's rate of overseas growth.

British, having assumed demand for the `proper' pattern would return to normal once the War was over, were not particularly worried.

But that was not to be. The Indian stick, having been found to have a number of advantages over the English design, gradually took over. The consequences are described in the Rules chapter. The most important was that it took almost twenty years to make some essential rule changes, a period during which the game virtually stood still.

Helsinki in 1952

Helsinki provided the first warning sign of G.B`s coming decline. Not too serious, but a bronze medal instead of a hoped for gold.

Participation had also resulted in a renewal of `Adherence' to the F.I.H. With the writing on the wall, it would still not have been too late to face facts and apply for full membership, the same as everyone else. But the Home Countries had to be different and, incidentally, pay the penalty of isolation - of not being able to take part in deliberations affecting the expanding role of the F.I.H. e.g. other tournaments, appointments of officials, committees and so on.

The pattern continued. At the Melbourne Olympics Great Britain, adhering still, again dropped a place to come 4th. More warning signs at Rome. Fourth again, but qualifying for the semi-finals only after winning in extra time.

There were a fair number of university graduates in the 1964 team at Tokyo. The Manager, a university don, suggested the way to win was to capitalise on their upbringing by playing a more tactical game. Unfortunately, their first opponents, a fit and physical Australian side had little respect for such refinements. In the opening stages a rising shot from a penalty corner - normally accepted at that time - badly injured the British goalkeeper.

The Aussies went on to an overwhelming victory of 7-0 with G.B. finishing 10th. Surprise was expressed about the aggresssive competitiveness displayed by many of the teams. The Manager commented in his report that `friendly' international matches among the Home Countries had little training value and for the future the business of winning needed to be studied as a primary objective.

It was not an auspicious year. By this time F.I.H. affiliations had increased to 52 national associations and in the light of such strength the Rules Board had to accede to pressure for their greater say - an increase in representation from 3 to 8 as opposed to 10 for the Home Countries.

At Mexico in 1968 G.B. were a disastrous 12th, coincident with which some expansionary plans of the F.I.H. came to fruition. The risks of hockey's Olympic exclusion were becoming minimal but, with easier travelling conditions and encouraged by the policy of their own representative body, the General Assembly of International Sports Federations, they had as a precaution had arrangements in train for other kinds of international tournaments e.g. World and Continental Cups. These now came into being. It meant the F.I.H. were home and dry - the Olympics were no longer their sole raison d`etre.

Over the same period increased feelings of competitiveness and frustration with poor Olympic performances had resulted in the leading London clubs taking the initiative into their own hands and deciding that from season 1969/70 they would have a league. The H.A. stood passively by. Other leagues were formed in the provinces. Stung, maybe, by a feeling that they were out of touch with their members, and in spite of it not being in keeping with their creed, each of the Home Countries then applied to participate in the first (1970) European Cup. Their track record did not merit selection for the first World Cup in 1971.

Facing the facts

The `No leagues, cups or prizes' rule had lasted since 1892. With the principle breached, with the F.I.H. widening their activities and gaining inexorably in influence, there was only one course left - to face the facts. What point was there now in denying oneself full F.I.H. affiliation? The Welsh, who seemed to have a greater appreciation of the situation, acted first and affiliated at the 1968 F.I.H. Congress in Mexico.

The decision upset the English and Scots because they realised, should the occasion arise, that the G.B. majority over the F.I.H. on the Rules Board of 10 to 8 would now become an 8 to 10 minority. Both Countries announced their determination not to affiliate. It was a gesture. They had no option. At the next Congress they too applied for membership and were accepted.

This account has tried hard - perhaps too hard - to explain an attitude which today`s generation may not easily understand. It had over the years been a stubborn, backs to the wall, resistance against the odds. In their fight for pure `amateurism' the elders of British hockey had outlasted their opposite numbers in rugby, football and cricket but the end was inevitable. Nationalism, the importance of winning, the growth of tournaments and the demand upon players in terms of fitness and training were the new yardsticks. Costs and commercialism became over-riding considerations. From then on it was accepted that competitiveness and the international shop window would have to take pride of place.

On reflection the postwar period had so far been a mixture of drift, muddle and confusion. For the British a slow decline, for the F.I.H. the long wait for their moment of take-over. For the game it had meant an absence of leadership with its public image deteriorating. Outdated rules had made umpiring difficult - too many grass pitches damp, heavy or inadequately cut had hampered the Indian stick potential for skilful play. There were insufficient financial resources. The only bright spot had been the bouyancy of the women's international tournaments under the enthusiastic management of the International Federation of Womens' Hockey Associations.

Competitiveness

But they, too, had been having problems and the time had come for them to be absorbed.

The introduction of the Indian stick led to more stick skill and competitiveness. Like their traditionally minded men, the English women were reluctant to change from what had always been regarded as the standard stick design. For a number of years it did not matter. Friendly pioneering with plenty of demonstration matches continued to be the main characteristic of the IFWHA tours with English superiority remaining strong enough for there to be no call for tournament champions. But gradually, the Americans, Dutch, Germans and Australians, by then, probably, all with Indian sticks, closed the gap and started to win. With the players wanting more and more to have winners, consider a brief recap of the overall situation.

In 1953 the growing strength of the IFW led the FIH to suggest a Joint Consultative Committee be formed to facilitate liaison and co-operation. The intention may in part have been to keep tabs on IFW activities because the latter expressed disappointment over the lack of discussion and a declining number of meetings.

In keeping with the world trend towards sex equality, the participation of women in Olympic sports - nil in 1896 - had been growing. At an I.O.C. Congress in 1970 a decision was taken to increase further the number of their events, implemented at the 1972 Congress in Munich by the addition of three more sports.

Women's hockey was also accepted in principle but its entry was deferred, due, it is understood, to the game's absence of integrated management. That concentrated the minds of the FIH for with the machinery of the Consultative Committee available for selection of the participating countries there was a prospect of the IFW's existence being perpetuated. The FIH thereupon discontinued the Committee.

They were persuaded to resume relationships in 1974 with a Supreme Council having four representatives from each group and a role of dealing with matters of common policy. But when in the same year the I.O.C. formally confirmed hockey's future Olympic participation - although deferred until 1980 pending an `etude special' of the management structure - the FIH again withdrew. Since they were the only body affiliated to the I.O.C. - and there could only be one for each sport - that meant the IFW were left high and dry.

The attraction and popularity of the IFW had been the social aspects of their conferences and tours. Even so with the changing trend towards nationalism and the importance of winning, there would now be little point in having two bodies with similar overall objectives.

At their 1975 Conference in Edinburgh, the I.F.W.H.A. resolved to become competitive and have a championship tournament. They also voted overwhelmingly in favour of Olympic participation. At the following Conference in Vancouver they upgraded their tournament to a World Championship, which may not have pleased the F.I.H.

But the die was cast. With F.I.H. membership the only channel for Olympic participation and their willingness to receive individual requests for affiliation from I.F.W.H.A. members, a questioning of the purpose of the latter`s continuing existence became inevitable. At Vancouver they reluctantly accepted the realities and decided the next Conference at Kuala Lumpur in 1983 should be their last, at which stage those members still unattached formally joined the FIH either directly or through their existing men`s Association. It was a sad ending to what had been a most successful and efficient body which had worked wonders in spreading the game for women overseas.

The take off

With an imminent revolution in the form of artificial pitches, sponsoring and wider television coverage, the F.I.H. take-overs marked a turning point. Play changed beyond recognition and, as in the world at large, progress reflected life's more material outlook.

Tournaments proliferated - World Cups, Champions Trophies, Continental Cups, Intercontinental Cups, Inter-Nations Cups, national under 21, under 18 and under 16 tournaments and generally both for men and women. It became `cups with everything'. National sides and their clubs, in ever increasing numbers of senior down to junior leagues, found themselves being awarded an embarrassment of cups and `gold', `silver' and bronze medals. Housing them became a problem.

With the help of artificial surfaces, games were more efficiently controlled by a more committed breed of umpires. There were plastic - and at last seamless - balls, more powerful sticks, greater goalkeeper protection, and to cap it all, at the 1984 Los Angeles Olympics, the introduction of instant world wide television combined with exclusive sponsorship. After sixty years of fluctuating fortunes it provided the I.O.C. with substantial funds.

A share was passed to the International Federations to give the F.I.H. among others the prospect at last of future financial stability.

Consolidation

The F.I.H. had now passed from childhood through adolescence to manhood but it still lacked maturity. During the build up Rene Frank had been dedicated and single minded with the Council dutifully rubber stamping his decisions. The need to update the game seems to have had a lower priory as witness the time it had taken to amend the rules following the adoption of the Indian stick.

With the smaller Associations, who formed the bulk of the membership, usually short of funds, lack of money had been a continuing handicap to administrative expansion. At one Congress an operating loss was declared. Deficits were announced at one or two others because of delays in the payment of affiliation fees. International tournaments had been held only because the host countries were willing to underwrite the cost. For example for the 4th World Cup in Buenos Aires the Argentina Association met the travel, board and lodging costs of 3 FIH officials, 2 technical delegates, some 6 jury of appeal, 20 umpires as well as 16 judges, plus 16 players and 3 officials per team.

Late in 1983, shortly before the Los Angeles Olympics, Frank died. Etienne Glichitch, the new President, started upon the next phase - of maturity: and he needed help rather than passive support.

The immediate question was what to do with the money from Los Angeles. With little accord at that time between North and South Korea, there was no knowing what surplus, if any, might arise from the Seoul Olympics in 1988. To avoid the temptation of overspending it was decided, sensibly, to treat most of the L.A. windfall as a capital item. The bulk was transferred to a newly formed Trust located in Switzerland, with part being used to purchase the freehold of the FIH administrative offices in Brussels.

A separate decision was to delegate work by giving greater autonomy and independence to the Continental Federations.

Next was the role of Council membership. At first they had been Association nominees. Later, when an electoral system was introduced, the results continued to reflect a geographic spread rather than a fund of experience and advice. (In making a long service award to one Council member, Glichitch commented with a disarming smile - and accepted as such because the example was not unique - that during his first ten years in office the recipient had never opened his mouth.)

As now, members held office for four years and were eligible for re-election. It was, therefore, going to take time for more experience to be injected, but that did not stop the new broom getting started with the setting up of a working party to review the situation, the outcome of which was a new Committee or two e.g. for Equipment and Umpires, and the introduction of new blood into some of the others.

Disappointingly, instead of turning to the broad development of the game, the Committees with fresh enthusiasm concentrated their energies on refining rules for the tighter control of major tournaments thus becoming involved in detail and piecemeal changes as described in the appropriate chapters. The overall effect was to make the game even less intelligible to the ordinary spectator and less attractive for T.V.

Few seemed to grasp the impact upon sports equipment of technological advances. Today, no golfer would expect to win a major tournament without the use of the most modern clubs and balls. The wooden frame of the tennis racquet has been discarded first in favour of metal, then for carbon fibre with a consequence of converting many a men`s singles from a game of skill to the monotony of superior serving power, although at Wimbledon in 1995 the L.T.A. did admittedly have the sense to lessen the effect by introducing softer balls.

A recent streamlining and resurfacing of the javelin helps it travel further through the air. The pole vaulter`s pole is a better example. Here wood has also been discarded, this time in favour of a combination of carbon fibre and metal which, with the help of NASA space programme technology, bends as the vaulter climbs it to break one more world record. Before use it is even modified by computer aided, critical path analysis to suit the height, strength and technique of the individual vaulter. (Vide -More than a Game: B.B.C. Books)

Stick manufacturers had joined in. Heads were laminated with different woods and handles made of fibre glass or of carbon and kevlar fibre bound with epoxy resin i.e. synthetic polymers used as structural plastics. The developments meant it was not only the players but the manufacturers who were competing.

At the present rate there can be little doubt that sticks will become even more powerful and in so doing expose the penalty corner defenders, especially the non-goalkeepers, to greater vulnerability.as for example at the Seoul Olympics where a penalty corner defender was hit on the head by a deflected ball of frightening speed and nearly killed. Helmets could soon become compulsory for them. The partial remedy chosen by the Rules Board was for the corner hit-out to be stopped outside the circle - not particularly practical for most of women`s hockey, for lower teams, children and those still playing on grass.

The Rules Board have now advanced the danger level a stage further by permitting teams to have rolling substitutes. The consequence for top teams is the use of a specialist `player'. He is not given much of a game, that does not seem to be important these days, for his sole task is the taking of penalty corner hits: and just as the pole vaulter`s pole is adjusted by critical path analysis to suit his height, strength and technique, so within three or four years might be the individually made stick of the corner hitter, who by that time could well be joined by a second specialist with the job of stopping the hit-out from the corner. The rule is of no practical use for the average team or for children; and such concentration on the sole objective of winning is a travesty of the original purpose of sport - the enjoyment of some form of healthy relaxation.

The obvious remedy, which will have to come sooner or later, is to call a halt and ban sticks beyond a particular degree of power, the simple dividing line, of course, being the use of anything other than wood.

PHIL APPLEYARD O.B.E.
H.A. President 1985 - 1995

All H.A. Presidents have been figureheads - men of stature and repute. Phil Appleyard was no exception but he had another asset - a man of initiative. His first role was to oversee the management of the 6th World Cup at Willesden in 1986. It was rated a great success. The games attracted more spectators than for any previous World Cup with the demand for tickets producing a black market. Realising the interest, the B.B.C. even changed its programme at short notice, substituting hockey for its standard Saturday afternoon high spot of soccer. A Veteran`s tournament drew 80 teams, 40 of them from overseas, while the ancillary programmes included displays at the ground, the purchase of the whole seating of a West End theatre and a number of special dinners. That was followed by groundwork for the setting up of a national H.Q. at Milton Keynes. He became a member of the F.I.H. Council and following the sudden death of its Honorary Treasurer accepted a request to take over that role starting immediately to re-organise the Federation`s financial housekeeping and produce more informative accounts. He was the obvious choice for the chairmanship of the F.I.H. Ad Hoc Committee to recommend what measures were necessary to bring the management of world hockey into the 20th century. The quality of the report speaks for itself.

Chapter 6

The Appleyard Committee, future outlook

By 1993, with work on the Seoul and Barcelona Olympics completed, the FIH had more breathing space and set up an `Ad Hoc' Committee under the chairmanship of Phil Appleyard to examine the Statutes and Bye-laws and adapt them to present day needs. Their report and recommendations were presented to the 70th Congress in November 1994 and approved.

The proposals included the establishment of an Executive Board `To convert the decisions of the Council into action' and a new appointment - that of Executive Director with responsibility for day to day management. The Committee also proposed Objectives and a Philosophy. They are worth being put on record.

Objectives

1. To ensure the F.I.H. is a representative body governing hockey in an efficient and democratic fashion.
2. To improve the efficiency and capability of the F.I.H. in introducing, developing and governing hockey.
3. To give the maximum opportunity and support to those endeavouring to further hockey in terms of both quality and quantity.
4. To maintain, improve and strengthen the position and image of hockey in the world of international sports.

Basic Philosophy

A. A more professional approach to its management but always bearing in mind the sport`s image and the importance of elected officers representing the F.I.H.
B. A broader debate in Congress in respect of F.I.H. policies and operations.
C. Greater participation in the deliberations of the Council.
D. A greater degree of accountability.
E. A greater spread of input and responsibility in the decision making process.
F. Committees having more effective and meaningful inputs.
G. Better communication both internally and externally.

The implication, and correctly so, was of an outdated, passive Council, although in mitigation one must remember the then pace of change and the legacy of Rene Frank`s personal dedication in pursuit of full F.I.H. control of the game. Item C - greater participation in deliberation - was re-inforced by a decision that each future candidate for Council election should provide a curriculum vitae. Item D led for the first time to the presentation at the Congress of full and open accounts prepared and issued by an international firm of Chartered Accountants.

If the objectives and philosophy are to be adopted, positive action is needed re-inforced, perhaps, by having the reports of the new Executive Director presented along similar lines. The sad alternative might be to see them end up as platitudes.

Time will tell, but a promising innovation at the 70th Congress was a discussion forum opened by Bob Davidzon, President of the Umpires` Committee, during which he illustrated the complications of current rules and umpiring including the too frequent blowing of whistles.

Summary

This brings the history up to the mid nineties. Next are some chapters about separate aspects, e.g. umpires, sticks, balls and artificial surfaces, but before that this seems to be an opportunity for a few comments about the directions in which the FIH might take the game.

Looking ahead

Enough, surely, has been written already to justify the claim made at the beginning of the book that the history of hockey is a romance. But what of the future?

Today major sports concentrate on their shop windows. Hockey may trail behind the leaders because complicated rules make it less attractive to watch. Even so, reference to any set of FIH minutes reveals the attitude is the same, maybe, even stronger.

Were it not for the prospects of a change following the Appleyard report, the outlook would not be particularly bright. Hockey, compared with football, rugby and cricket, had by 1994 become the most bureaucratic sport with some 90 pages* of rules and explanations, with another 100 odd pages of a Technical Manual for international tournaments, the numerous officials required for running them, the detailed Statutes and Byelaws and the meticulous equipment definitions.

The reason sprang from the unusual history of the game`s management which had started in the normal way from the grass roots upwards with club representatives having a major influence upon development.

*Reduced now to 62 pages with a `More user friendly edition'

Progress was then interrupted by the setting up of the F.I.H. solely to run the Olympics and, later, World tournaments. For some 45 years they performed an effective job during which period their lack of interest for the grass roots, then being looked after by the British, was not critical.

However, once they widened their powers and acquired full control of the game, the situation changed. It meant their responsibilities now included the rules: and they were applicable to all players. But the Olympic outlook was so ingrained that -a fear expressed at the time by Mark Cowlishaw, the then Secretary of the Board - the need for an FIH change of perspective was not realised. They continued to legislate from and for the top, as instanced by the present complicated penalty corner rule.

In the light of today`s attitudes to sport, there would seem to be no reason to expect any changes were it not for the hope of a more motivated and efficient Council made aware by Appleyard`s Committee of their wider role - something the new Congress forums should help remind them must never be regarded as passive.

Synthetic Surfaces

A particular need is a drive for more synthetic surfaces (S.S.), to improve the game both for players and spectators.

Besides providing a better game, the surfaces are hard wearing and virtually free from climatic interference. In terms of use one additional pitch is equivalent to four of grass - a most important advantage in areas of high population density. They provide better facilities both for children, who then want to go on playing after their schooldays, and to lower team members who for similar reasons want to extend their playing years.

Given an adequate supply, the number of hockey players could double to produce much more press interest and T.V. coverage and a sizeable increase in FIH affiliation fees and status.

In today`s material world with television, videos and video games; with more one parent families, with countries internally, internationally or religiously at war; with poverty, drugs, political upheavals and so on, one might claim such a projection is a pipe dream. But, with the help of a motivated and better qualified Council, progress could surely be made because, so far, the FIH have done little apart from laying down minimum S.S. standards for international tournaments. The leading national Associations have in turn required S.S. usage for their top leagues but, apart from occasional support from various national authorities, progress has been disappointing with the exceptions of England, which has been fortunate to receive a lot of government support, and Holland. Between them these two countries probably have half the total world supply.

The official S.S. handbook simply states that the primary objective of the FIH is to ensure international competitions are conducted on suitable surfaces of optimum playing conditions subject to mimimum approved standards which are then set out. There is no exhortation for a maximum possible changeover from grass pitches: and the shock comes when one analyses the statistics.

Artificial pitches were first laid down in 1975. A quoted world total of around 1500 as at 1994 is almost certainly an underestimate: but assuming there were roughly 2000 after 20 years, it means that the average rate of installation for the 110 countries affiliated to the FIH was less than one new pitch per country per year - or less than half a pitch if England and Holland are excluded.

No-one can deny the serious burden of the cost but nor can one question the marked superiority of the new surfaces. So why not set up a sub-Committee to study the problem and make recommendations about what action to take - where to go for sources of finance and what influence the FIH might exert, e.g. with Olympic Solidarity, with the Continents via their Federations, even directly, if necessary, with separate countries. An investigation of the manufacturing side could follow. With scope for it becoming a several billion pound industry there has to be some prospect for negotiating special, bulk or local terms. More research might find cheaper materials.

Given initiative, substantial growth does not have to be a pipe dream. Many years ago some school Old Boys on the east coast of South Africa, who wanted a hockey pitch, were offered some wholly unsuitable, uneven waste land. They clubbed together to purchase a second hand earth mover, spent their week ends levelling the surface, seeded it and ended up with a highly presentable pitch and an earth mover for sale.

To save part of the costs could not a model `Do It Yourself' scheme be prepared for clubs of similar initiative - and especially if they were fortunate enough to have a qualified surveyor among their members - say to encourage them to lay the basic foundations? More synthetic surfaces would undoubtedly do hockey and the youth of the world a power of good. The author had prepared a report for the F.I.H. in 1987 on the general subject of artificial surfaces which covered many of the above points but the time was inopportune because, following Rene Frank's death, the Council were too involved with reviewing the work of the Committees. Regardless of how accurate the projections are proving to be, an extract - Appendix 5 - may still be found of interest.

The above is but one subject. There are others already mentioned which need to be discussed by future forums e.g. the power of the stick. It will in the end be a question of whether the FIH has the wisdom to put the development of the game and it's poor television and spectator image before top tournament `progress' and the pressure to see more and more goals.

A useful start could be made by reversing the status of the Technical and Development Committees. That accorded to the former has been unnecessarily important. The Development Committee, an ineffectual group with almost nothing to show for its existence, should be vitalised and given responsibility for producing more artificial pitches as well as control of the Equipment Committee.

The FIH carry a great responsibility and have a duty to lead. With their hands having been full these last ten or fifteen years, they have made some notable strides forward. Yet there is still a lot of rethinking to do along the lines of the Appleyard report and they need support, good wishes, and sustained pressure to ensure the good work continues.

Chapter 7

The Rules

Laying the foundations

Using the model of football, when Teddington set up goals of similar size and started hitting a cricket ball with home made sticks, all that was needed in 'rules' terms was broad agreement about the area of the pitch, the goals, the number of players and the period of play. The detail might have varied from week to week but as the pattern settled subsequent changes were recorded in a minute book. The earliest record of a complete set was that published when Richmond, supported by Surbiton, organised the first Association in 1875.

A copy of these rules appears in Appendix 1. The first feature to note is the absence of a reference to umpires. They were not needed because if a player broke a rule he would stop. Nor is there any reference to penalties because there were no deliberate fouls. If there was doubt about an incident ranking as an infringement, there would be an appeal which the captains would resolve.

With the interest of other clubs waning, Teddington went on refining their rules. Other clubs copying the game might have a rule or two of their own (Gifford, a famous centre forward of the Molesey Club continued to use a one-handed stick): but the initiative stayed with Teddington and formed the basis of an updated version when Wimbledon in turn, took the lead in setting up the present H.A. in 1886. It contained more detail with 19 sections in place of the previous 12.

The main changes were:-
(1) Recognition of the circle as described in the general narrative and the practical consequence, when the ball went over the goal-line, of having a bully at 25 yards.
(2) Reducing the goal to its present size.
(3) A reference to the role of umpires who had now begun to be appointed.
(4) A free hit instead of a bully for infringements.

Apart from introducing the crucial rule banning leagues and games for cups or prizes in 1892 the tendency, except for refinements, was then to leave the rules alone.

An International Rules Board
With clubs being formed in Ireland, Wales and Scotland and the start of

A. FRAMPTON Teddington and England

It is doubtful whether anyone contributed more than `Fram' to the establishment of the game. He was a born organiser.

A friend had persuaded him to join Teddington in 1889 to try out the newly introduced role of goalkeeper. He next came to the fore in the business world when the Companies Act of 1896 introduced share capital and limited liability. It resulted in the dealing system on the Stock Exchange of which he became a popular member, sufficiently so that, when the quality of his goalkeeping led to his being capped, the Exchange organised a ceremony at which he was formally presented with his shirt badge of a red rose.

In 1899 he was appointed the H.A. Secretary. To ensure all countries played to the same rules, one of his early tasks was to create an International Rules Board, of which he also became Secretary. A further move was to centralise umpiring starting with the setting up of the Southern Counties Hockey Umpires Association of which he became President.

In his spare time he acted as Club Treasurer and President.

international matches, the next stage was to co-ordinate national variations in play (an Irish team for example consisted of twelve players) by agreeing in 1900 to a common code under the control of an International Rules Board. The copyright of the rules vested originally with the H.A. It was transferred to the Rules Board itself in the 1950`s and today comes under the jurisdiction of the F.I.H. (Over the years the body has had a change or two in title so for the sake of simplicity it has been referred to throughout the book as the Rules Board)

Amendments and representation

Once a base was established, the typical British reluctance to tamper with the rules took over. There was, for example, one irritating feature which permitted an opponent to hook the stick of a player as he went to hit the ball. Another, a relic of poor grounds, allowed the stopping of the ball with the foot. Neither was abandoned until well after the first War.

The main pre-occupation was Board representation. Ireland and Scotland were particularly unhappy that the Hockey Association, who, admittedly, had at least ten times as many players, retained for too long a controlling vote. At one stage they withdrew, but since the Board rarely met - gaps between meetings would exceed a year - the gesture had little practical significance with a banding together again once external considerations e.g. the formative period of the F.I.H., required a combined approach.

Growth and affiliations

Overseas there was a growing interest in the game and a wish to take it up. The H.A. received a number of requests for copies of the rules and affiliation, which in practical terms meant being put on the mailing list for details of future changes. It led to no wish on the part of G.B. to set up a wider body hence the abortive Hamburg meeting in 1912 when a proposal to have a European group foundered over the no cups or prizes principle.

Similarly with the F.I.H. The British recognised the wish of their affiliated Associations to compete in the Olympics but, since they were just a small sector of the hockey playing community and the event took place once only every four years, there was no thought in the early years of regarding that as a reason for accepting FIH representation.

Nevertheless, as the Federation grew they exerted more pressure for membership. The H.A. accepted that France and Belgium were nominally responsible for the rules of the game in their respective countries, but the only other concession they would make was to agree to keep the F.I.H. informed about any intended changes and consider any rule recommendations the F.I.H. might wish to propose. Until 1947 the Board would go no further. In their view the F.I.H. were simply a part of the organisational process for Olympic participation.

However, in 1947, when G.B. hockey was forced to participate in the 1948 Olympics and thus had to join the F.I.H., the latter were, at last, able to demand in return Rules Board membership. It was duly conceded. Some sixteen years later, after continuing British Olympic participation and more F.I.H. growth, the representation was increased. It led to no real change. The two groups with different outlooks appeared wary of each other.

Impact of Indian Sticks

It was a poor reflection upon the responsibility and judgement of both parties for it covered the period of the introduction of the Indian stick.

The obvious problem which considerably lessened the enjoyment of playing, was a marked increase when hitting the ball of raising the stick above the shoulder - a then infringement. Whereas the more rounded arc of a hit with the English stick made it comparatively easy to conform to the rule, the vertical trajectory needed for the Indian stick required a much more disciplined stroke. (See diagrams on P.25) With practice most players could learn not to go above the top of the head but the distance between that and the shoulder was a source of frustration, especially at a short corner, because the umpire's decision reflected not only his judgement at the margin, but its consistency relative to that of his opposite number. Human nature being what it is, variations were inevitable.

There was a simple remedy - to amend the rules: but with the British Rules Board members of that time never themselves having used such a stick plus the slow rate of its adoption within the U.K., there was an insufficient awareness of the need. One would have expected the F.I.H. to exert more pressure for change, but they remained fairly much at arms length from the rest of the Rules Board. If anything, their greater concern was to complete the closing stages of their long haul towards overall control of the game.

The rule was abolished eventually in 1959 but, with the grass pitches of the day varying in quality, the unrestricted hit was considered too dangerous. In 1967 the rule was restored, to be abandoned finally some ten years later because of two new factors - more sophisticated materials, such as glass fibre shafts which by imparting more power lessened the need for full swings and the advent of artificial surfaces over which ball propulsion was much smoother.

Another difficulty was the bully. The circumstances of its replacement, delayed until 1959, were referred to earlier in the body of the book and given in detail in Appendix 2.

There remained the roll-in which had produced too much bunching and stick interference. It was superceded, first by the push-in and later the hit.

So, at last, far too long after its introduction, the superior advantages of the Indian stick could be fully exploited. Prevarication had left the game standing still for almost twenty years.

Change of accent and control

When, between 1968 and 1970, the Home Countries applied separately for direct F.I.H. affiliation instead of their previous combined G.B. "adherence", the Rules Board, although ostensibly remaining independent, at length came under effective F.I.H. control and the clog of tradition disappeared. Since then the Board have followed an active policy with a programme of regular meetings. Three distinct phases have tested them.

Increased competition

First was the introduction of World and Continental tournaments which brought about a notable increase in competitiveness and nationalism and led to stricter control and the introduction of cards for warnings and suspensions. Substitutes were allowed with offside being eased by having two defenders instead of three.

Artificial surfaces

The free running and easily stopped ball on artificial surfaces produced the next phase of changes - banning a newly devised chip shot, a ball lifted into the circle, and some new types of sticks; limiting offside to a 25 yard distance from the goal-line, and stricter control against physical contact and the taking of free hits within 5 yards of the circle - remedies quickly applied and for which the Rules Board deserve full marks.

Commercialism

Sponsorship and the growth of commercialism produced other changes and continue to do so e.g. the rules for substitutes and the complications of the penalty corner illustrated at the forum of the 70th Congress with Bob Davidzon`s account of six types of hit into the goal half of which were allowable and half not.

Overall effect

Until 1994 the measures were piecemeal. No thought seemed to be given to the accumulating complications of the rules and their effect upon the ordinary player, upon the television picture and the understanding of the spectator, problems referred to earlier in the `Looking ahead' summary and which the post Appleyard FIH Council will need to study and seem already to be doing so

Statutes and Bye-laws

There is another set of rules - those which set up and regulate the F.I.H. constitution.

In their original 1924 form they stated the title of the Federation, named the President, Secretary and Treasurer, the members attending and the seven initial national Associations which they represented. As an I.O.C. requirement there was added a definition of an amateur hockey player. The total content occupied less than a page and was regarded as adequate by the Olympic Committee.

Amendments were made from time to time until 1947 when the FIH campaign to acquire full control of the game and its rules took off. The policy followed was to assume power, always in writing, at every opportunity.

It came to fruition when the introduction of World and Continental tournaments as additions to the Olympic role provided more than sufficient ammunition. The result was a constitution much greater in detail than that thought necessary by the corresponding bodies of cricket, football and rugby. Today the document consists of 21 Statutes, many with several sub-sections, 19 general Bye-laws and another 14 relating to the Continental Federations. They include, for example, two official languages, two definitions of Continental Federations, a definition of Field hockey and a specific authority to `control the game', something, for example, not thought necessary in their day by the IFWHA whose simple objective was `to further its best interests`.

This is not particularly important compared with the achievement of the FIH in securing hockey`s inclusion in the Olympic Games nor has it much, if any, effect upon the average player who is probably unaware such Statutes and Byelaws exist.

Chapter 8

Umpiring

An Olympic Final

The end of four hard years of training and sacrifice. The last whistle blows; a perfunctory handshake by some for the umpires who then fade from the scene. The losers look philosophic. The winners erupt into euphoria.

'What of the game? Well, it took it's course. The winners just about deserved the gold. You'll find the usual details in tomorrow's papers - an outstanding player or two, the goalscorers, the goalkeeping and so on. Yes - the teams were clearly tensed up to start with but they settled down alright although one must admit, with only a goal in it, the last quarter of an hour was very exciting - touch and go all the way. The umpires? No, no-one mentioned them. There was no need to really. They performed their required role. An odd card, perhaps, but nothing special.'

Yet when one comes to think about the importance of the occasion and the team tensions which seemed to evaporate, the umpires must have done rather a good job, especially with the speed of today's games and the scope for things to happen out of sight. Let's reflect more.

Modern standards

Umpires operating at this level are as skilled as the players they control: efficient, consistent, each working closely with his colleague at the other end.

Off duty during the tournament they watch team tactics as well as the players for their skills, foibles, and infringements. Each evening, guided by their manager, they analyse and discuss problems which may arise, for the result of the tournament, the glory of a gold medal, could so easily rest upon one instantly taken decision which these days would very rarely be wrong. Not unpredictably, the better they perform, the more they are taken for granted. The reward? Satisfaction for a job well done, a pat on the back from the manager and congratulations from the closely knit community of their colleagues.

How do they get appointed? Experience accumulated as they rise through the ranks. Recommended by their Country, graded, sent on training courses, tested and tried. Then the tournament. Nothing left to chance. The manager puts them through their paces to make sure they are fit, followed, once the games start, by his daily inquests, assessments, advice etc. as explained above. Their future will depend upon how they respond which is why they fraternise these

An umpire's dress

In the earliest days dress reflected the status and limits of the umpire's role. In this North team of 1894 the umpire wears a top hat, an overcoat having an astrakhan collar but with trousers rolled up to avoid any mud. He would be seated and have the sole role of interpreting on appeal whether or not a rule had been infringed. He had no whistle.

Once umpires became active their dress eventually changed to standard flannel trousers, blazer, shirt, collar and tie. It was not until after the heat of the Mexico Olympics of 1968 that a shirt with an open collar was permitted and many years later that the uniform of coloured shirts distinct from those of the players were introduced.

days only with each other: not from aloofness, but because of their concentration on a serious objective - an unblemished performance.

The higher umpires go, the more they have to learn, apply themselves and be exemplars for others. They must know their guidance notes inside out. Nor is it just a knowledge of the rules. With the speed of the game on artificial surfaces they have to be fit, not only physically but in judgment and mental re-action.

Today, top umpires are taught not to get involved with the players - neither during the game nor after; to be deaf to remarks on the pitch unless, of course, someone goes over the top. To develop their own personality, flair and control; not to penalise the trivial but to let the game flow by allowing as much advantage as possible.

To achieve, in other words, a highly skilled professional standard, which because of the pace and intensity of the game is superior to that required for tennis, soccer, rugby or cricket which do, of course, have distinct pressure areas of their own. It is a standard seldom appreciated or recognised fully either by the Press, the players or their supporters, wrapped up as they usually are almost wholly in the result.

All a far cry from the beginning - so far, in fact, that to describe the early days to the modern player may seem like bathos. Here is a go.

The pattern developed somewhat along these lines. A start without umpires followed by a volunteer, whistleless, supporter agreeing to act as a judge of appeal - not of an infringement but of a rule interpretation. The next stage was umpires with whistles assisted by the players, who would stop or point out their own unnoticed infringements - a practice which continued up to the beginning of the last War.

Finally the more serious stage including the takeover of international control by the F.I.H., the issue of guidance notes and with grading and coaching leading to the standards of today.

The beginning

With simple rules and the co-operation of the players umpiring within a club was easy. The difficulties began when clubs started to play each other for they would not necessarily have identical rules or apply them in the same way. So there would be pre-match discussions about interpretations with captains giving a decision should any questions be raised during play. As skills increased, and to leave the captains freer, independent arbiters began to be appointed: and because the first players were cricketers and decisions were made on appeal, they were designated `umpires' rather than referees. They had no whistles.

This did not mean a rapid growth in umpiring. There had been no provision for appointments in the rules of the 1875 Hockey Association nor was there a specific requirement in the first rules of today's Association set up in 1886. They merely stated that, if there were no umpires, the captains should decide any disputes on appeal.

But, not unexpectedly, the practice of umpiring began to increase. It was helped, curiously, by the 'No cups or prizes' attitude, for with results having only token significance, the typical umpire was able to be a volunteer, attracted by the opportunity of a friendly, enjoyable afternoon and a feeling, perhaps, that in a modest way he would be contributing to the pleasure of the game. It was not a difficult job - just to be asked for a ruling which would always be accepted.

The first 30 years

The system of playing with a mixture of voluntary stoppings and appeals lasted nearly thirty years at which stage common sense began to take over. The first step was a minor rule change in 1897 requiring an umpire, in the event of an incorrect roll-in or bully, to act on his own authority and blow for a retake. Two years later Wimbledon wrote a letter to the magazine 'Winter Sports' proposing that umpires should take active control as in rugby and soccer. When the Rules Board was set up in 1900 to establish a consistent code for the Home Countries, it still retained the appeal procedure but added a recommendation that umpires should take the initiative and blow.

(The Irish who had had leagues from the outset, must surely have used whistles. Around this early period the minutes of the League Committee of the Leinster Branch contain records of club appeals against match results, some of which were accepted, on the grounds of the umpire's lack of knowledge of the rules).

The first Umpires Association

In those years there was no thought of training, coaching or grading - it was probably considered unnecessary. Frampton when he set up the Rules Board did try without support to organise what was called a Referees' Association. (A referee was used for some of the more important matches to decide any differences between umpires, to record the score and keep the time - rather like the modern technical delegate). He had more success in 1905 with the active help of Hopperton of the Dulwich Club. Between them they persuaded the Southern clubs to have an Umpires Association controlled by a committee of their choosing. Frampton became the President. The Southern Counties and the H.A. had no objections to such a body for umpire recruitment or club match appointments, but they were certainly not going to allow them to make appointments in their region for important fixtures such as Divisional and International matches.

These major games - followed always by formal dinners - were regarded as privileged social occasions, the preserve of top officials. The S.C.H.U.A. did eventually obtain recognition from the South in 1911 because a majority of their officials were members of both bodies. They had to wait until 1923, again helped by dual representation, for the H.A. to accept them.

As it happens, there still exists a letter written in 1912 on Bath Club notepaper by a top official of the H.A. sympathising with Cambridge University about the attitude of the S.C.H.U.A. co-incident with which was an article in the Westminster Gazette by an S.C.H.U.A. member making the comment that in spite of meeting demands at short notice for help during the season, no member of the S.C.H.U.A. had ever been asked to umpire the Varsity match "but in their place officials of the H.A. have officiated - and very badly too at that".

Post-war

The pleasant occupation of the average umpire changed little up to the last War. Post-war it began to be confusing, as, maybe, will this explanation, for it involves three sectors - the sticks, the rules and the umpires. The chapter on sticks sets out the problem, this one describes how the umpires coped, while the rules chapter offers reasons for the delay in making some necessary alterations.

The crux of the problem was the time it took for the British to change over from the English type of stick to the Indian design. The latter led to an improvement in stick skills and greater competitiveness. For more than ten years both types of stick were being used in the same match. The Indian stick justified the use of different rules. Only one set could be used and while players in other countries were making a rapid changeover, the traditional British, controllers of the rules, were too slow off the mark. It was the umpires who had to cope with the consequences.

Guidance notes

To lessen confusion, Mark Cowlishaw, Secretary of the Rules Board, added guidance notes to the rules. There had previously been a few definitions and explanations but these notes went into more detail and have since become a valuable feature of the Rules booklet - an umpire`s vade mecum which should be required reading for every serious player.

Coping with competitiveness

Greater competitiveness was displayed in other ways. Here are two examples. At the Helsinki Olympics in 1952 the sticks of one European country were noticeably in excess of the official 2 inch circumference. These were the days when every male carried a penknife to sharpen his pencil. Out they came to pare the sticks down to regulation size with international umpires required thereafter to carry an official test ring. Even they had to be adjusted. The edges were right

MARK COWLISHAW

Mark Cowlishaw was a highly efficient umpire.

He joined the Rules Board in 1939 and from 1947 until 1971 combined the posts of Chairman and Secretary. He was a vice-President both of the FIH and the Hockey Association and realised, long before the HA, that it was inevitable with the rapid growth of the game that a World Federation had to become established. From its modest beginnings the FIH gradually assumed this role with Cowlishaw almost the lone British supporter.

He officiated at 7 Olympics, 5 as an umpire including the final at Melbourne in 1956. The whistle he used on that occasion is in the H.A. museum.

angled and, as someone pointed out, it meant inadequate tolerance as the ring was passed round the bend of the stick. Today, the insides of rings are rounded.

The second instance relates to a lowering of fair play standards. In 1963 the guidance notes for rule 19 included the comment `if an umpire is in doubt concerning a decision, he may make such enquiry, i.e. of the player, as may be necessary to make a decision or correct one already made`. The note was withdrawn some time after 1970. A dilemma during an international match between two keen European rivals illustrates why.

A forward apparently hit the ball into the net whereupon the umpire awarded a goal. The other side protested. The umpire spoke briefly to the forward and then signalled a 16 yard hit. After the game the manager of the first team asked his forward what had happened. The account went something like this. `He asked me whether I actually contacted the ball with my stick as it came into the circle.' `What did you say?', `No'. The manager, once an international of the old school had through hard experience become a realist. He re-acted by saying `Look here, if he had any doubts, he had his other umpire to consult. If you do that again, you`ll no longer play for the side'.

The period coincided roughly with the F.I.H.`s introduction of green, yellow and red cards to signify warnings or degrees of suspension. One reason was said to be an aid to language problems. A decline in player attitudes would have been nearer the mark. There would have been little, if any, call for cards before the War.

Grading

When, reluctantly, the H.A. entered the league arena, they began to grade their umpires more strictly. (The A.E.W.H.A. with typical efficiency had introduced grading many years earlier.) The peak standard was an F.I.H. grading. Having first been recommended by the national Association, the qualification required for a badge was to officiate in a mimimum of three independent international matches and be awarded a `satisfactory` rating for each.

Inevitably, these first F.I.H. appointments fell into geographic pools but, since the range and quality of hockey throughout the world was wide, it meant those who gained badges were of mixed ability. They were sooner or later invited to international tournaments and given appointments for early round matches so that they could be monitored by the Technical Delegate and then either `rested` at an appropriate stage or persevered with. The latter could hope for a minimum five more games and, if satisfactory, receive the award of a Class 1 grading. The best would progress further to an Olympic/World Cup grade. Subject to revised age and fitness limits, this has remained the broad pattern.

Umpiring as a science

When Cowlishaw retired from his umpiring work, two F.I.H. officials, Lathouwers and McIldowie, took over the role. Nationalism and keenness to win had developed to such an extent that umpiring was now becoming a demanding, thankless, yet challenging job with a number of the old school giving up because of the aggressiveness of the players. Over an awkward transitional period their rethinking of the role - and at last more concentrated coaching and instruction - achieved wonders for their protegees.

The umpire and commercialism

The 1984 Los Angeles Olympics with its accent on commercialism led to more professional standards.

To protect the financial return, image and spectator appeal became more critical which meant greater responsibility being put upon the controllers of the game. A year or two later, one therefore finds an Umpires` Committee being introduced into the FIH structure with the Committee in turn deciding to appoint Umpire Managers for major international tournaments. It has been this Committee and their managers who have been responsible for the current quality of Olympic umpiring. Here is an example.

Around 1990/91 a major revision was made to the obstruction rule, a problem of the game from its earliest days. In the past changes had simply been published together with any necessary explanation of their application. On this occasion there was an umpire`s seminar at which Graham Nash, a leading umpire, explained the change.

He discussed it from the angle of a player receiving the ball both when he was stationary and when he was moving; the different directions he might be facing on its receipt, the direction in which he then moved off, according to the different positions and subsquent movements of a tackler and or his stick -and both in relation to his timing and apparent intentions and whether any resulting obstruction might be actual or implied.

That was just to begin with. Having stressed that under the rules they enjoyed a considerable degree of delegated authority, e.g. of interpretation, he gently threw in a reminder that there had to be consistency of interpretation not only with a partner during the game, but with all the other umpires officiating at the same tournament. A similar depth of analysis was given to other items discussed at the seminar. Few players are aware such studies take place.

The umpire`s duties do not rest there. He has to make himself readily visible to the spectator, the camera and the rest of the media, His signals must be clear and simple enough for everyone to understand. He must keep the teams fully under control, ensure the game flows and minimise delays from injuries and substitutions. He is no longer there for pleasant relaxation, to help out with the game and afterwards join in with the gossip, the reminiscences and his turn with the next round of drinks. Perhaps players can now understand the reasons for his lack of involvement with the players and the closeness of today`s umpiring fraternity.

95

Original FIH umpire`s badge - awarded only for the Olympics

Today`s FIH badge. Although the design retains the Olympic rings the wearer is not necessarily an Olympic umpire. The addition of a Crown denotes a Class 1 grade.

A much sought after FIH award, the Gust Lathouwers medallion -presented at each Congress to the umpire considered to have contributed most to the game.

CHAPTER 9

THE STICK

Over the years hockey has changed enormously. A major factor has been the development of the stick. It is doubtful whether any other item of sports equipment can have had such an impact, viz the change from the one handed form to the two handed, the `holly' and its consequences, the introduction of the spliced stick, which saved the game from extinction, the Indian pattern and the sophisticated sticks of today. Each change led to important advances. Nowadays a player probably takes his stick for granted. An account of its progression may help him to appreciate it more.

The earliest sticks were pieces of wood cut from a convenient tree. For their games Blackheath and others had used a one handed stick, the " weapon with a bent knob or hook at the end, large or small, thick or thin, according to the option of the player". The description `weapon' was not wholly inappropriate.

For use with a softish ball, the type of wood was probably not important but play with the heavier cricket ball required a more controlled action with a two handed stick, curved at the base and being rounded if necessary by levering after immersion in water for which the Secretary of the newly formed H.A. offered the following advice:-

`Use an ordinary maple stick. Put one end in boiling water for twenty minutes and then place it under a heavy vice to bend it out. Then, when dry and cold, spoke shave down until the face is like this (here followed a diagram of the striking face) generally sawing off a slice first. Then spoke shave the handle until it is a little over an inch in diameter at the top. The top of the handle and the face should be roughed with a coarse file.'

Other favoured woods were ash, oak and crab. Although there was an abundance of chestnut around the Bushy Park area it was generally considered too soft.

In keeping with his analytical mind, Battersby, referred to later in the `Balls' chapter, wrote some 18 pages on such aspects as the varieties of wood, the best shapes and the graining.

A keenness to experiment resulted in players having more than one stick. As the old ones were discarded, someone would usually gather them together for spare club use. A well known collection, some of which survive to this day, and all over a hundred years old, were those held by Comber of Trinity College. And who knows? One may have been used by the Duke of Clarence.

No stick was ideal. An advantage would usually be offset by a disadvantage. A hard hit would sting or break the stick. The curve at the bottom might make it difficult for dribbling or stopping the ball, if not on the right then on the left.

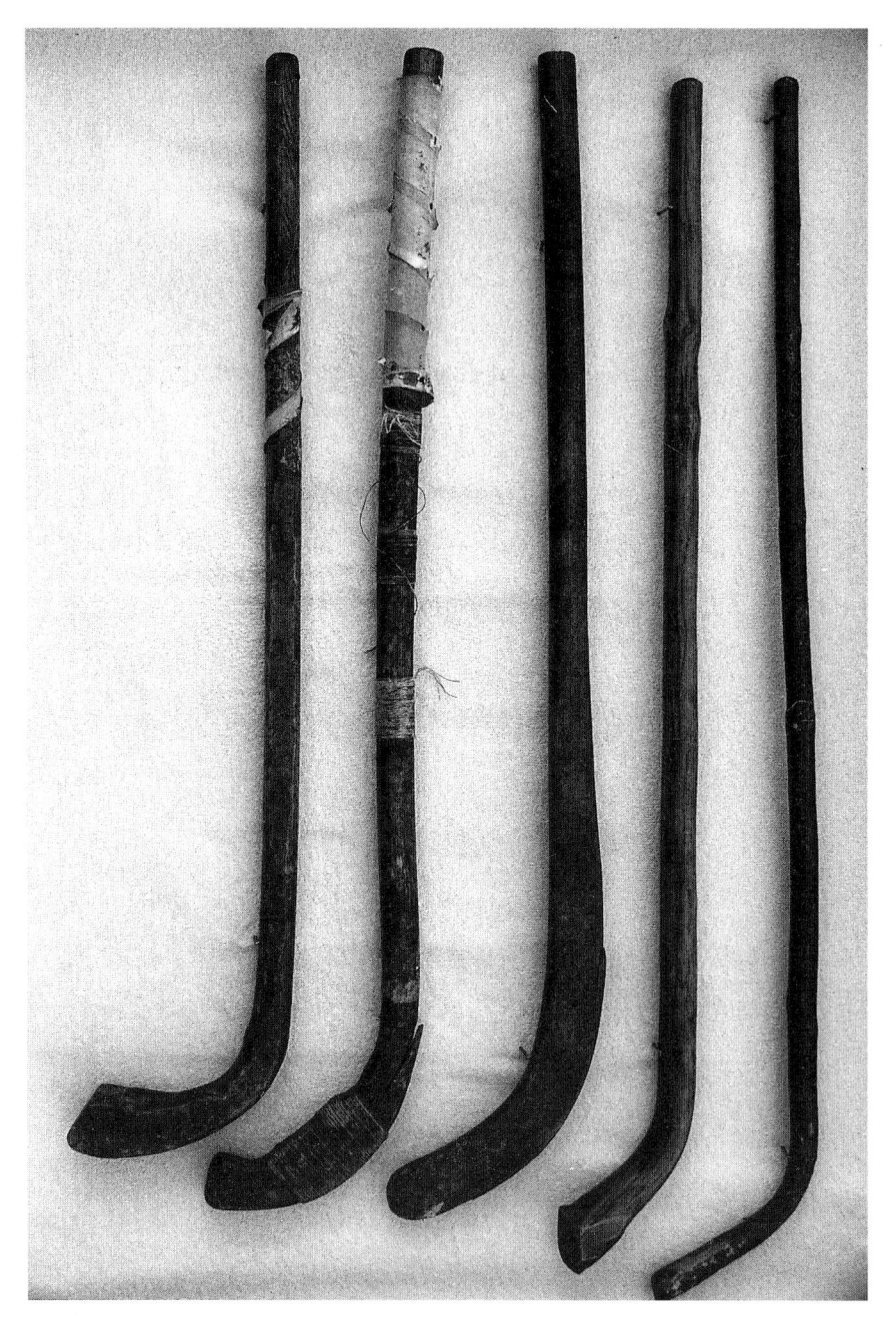

Sticks from the Comber collection - all over 100 years old. The Duke of Clarence may have used one

None of this really mattered to the Teddington players. Having devised a new game, they had the stimulus of discussing and working on its continuing development. The sting was reduced with bindings of leather, cloth or twine - or by wearing gloves. The stopping problem was helped by allowing a player to use his foot or hand. Reverse side play was simply banned. It was not quite the same for the other clubs. They were following a pattern someone else had laid down and the disadvantages of the sticks tempted some of them to revert to the Union game.

The search for a satisfactory stick went on. Hopes of solving two of the problems arose when someone discovered the whippiness of holly and its lack of sting. But they were dashed when it led to another extreme - the 'pernicious' long hits resulting, as already explained, in the introduction of the bully and the circle. Fortunately with a lack of supply of the wood not everyone was able to acquire it. But it was one more stage in the evolutionary process and with perseverance the players were beginning to get a feel of the game they were looking for.

The answer was found when Slazengers introduced their spliced stick in 1886. The description was 'a manufactured stick with a piece of wood glued on to the bend', designed, presumably, from their experience with spliced cricket bats. With the thinner blade many of the early versions used to break but the manufacturers got it right in the end. It revolutionised the game and ended competition from the Hockey Union which then folded up.

As the production of the new sticks got under way, the blades were made wider to help ball stopping. (They must have become too wide for the H.A. took the step of reducing what had been a rough and ready - though seldom tested - rule of a maximum 2_ inches circumference to 2 inches). The handles were of cane and the heads of ash. Other types of wood were discarded. From 1894 reverse side play began to be permitted but it was seldom tried because of the difficulty of control and the likelihood of the umpire blowing for obstruction. To make reverse side stopping easier one fashion in the early thirties was an angled toe - a trend which had to be halted because the point became dangerous.

Some useless information

Several years ago the Department of Scientific and Industrial Research commissioned a survey of woods used in the sports goods industry. A hundred and six varieties were examined. The sole use recorded for holly was as one of an assortment of types employed for the decorative design of billiard cue splices. What a sad relegation to virtual obscurity for a wood which once, though briefly, had such a vital impact on the game, one consequence of which - the circle - has remained in use ever since.

The sticks remained substantially in this `English' form for over fifty years, although there were regular refinements, e.g. the cane handles were interleaved with rubber, the splicing was improved and the head became laminated. A full stroke began to have a feeling of rhythm although it had nowhere near the power, which can be imparted these days into a modern stick. Dribbling skills continued to develop but they were elementary compared with those acquired later with the Indian stick. The secret of the abilities of legendary figures such as Shoveller and Dhyand Chand (Photographs show he was still using an English stick for the 1936 Olympics) was undoubtedly elusiveness and body swerve. Typically, the ball would be stopped suddenly by a stick hold on the top followed by a quick tap and acceleration.

The Indian stick

The Indian stick was the next stage. The origins seem reasonably certain. Hockey had been introduced by the Armed Forces and British Civil administrators. The Indian upper classes took to the game slowly but the ordinary Indian did not join in until around 1920. The standard sticks came from Britain. Then India started to make some of their own. They had no ash and it was too expensive for them to import. But there was plenty of mulberry which could be rounded more easily. Here is some background about the sticks of that time from Ferroze Khan, a veteran Olympian of 1928.

'My first contact with a regular stick was when I joined Lahore College in 1922. This stick known as a 'Dunda' was of pressed mulberry and of one whole piece, with woven cloth called Navar wrapped around the solid handle to minimise the sting to the hand that followed a hard hit. Most of the poor players used it before going in for the sophisticated hockey stick. At that time a Dunda cost 10 to 12 annas while the regular sticks could cost up to 5 rupees.

At the schools for the more prosperous there was hockey only for the senior classes: the lower class students had no participation in such games. The boys from the suburbs of the cities had their own manipulated sticks made from the branches of teak trees with the hockey stick curve. Village hockey was played with these sticks and a home made ball called a Khuddo. In my school days I played with this hockey gear."

He then refers to the introduction of the splice confirming that since ash favoured by the British was rare and expensive the Indian manufacturers used mulberry.

They found it difficult to copy the length of the curve so reduced it to about 7 or 8 inches - which although some 2 inches less than the English stick was still twice as long as the stick which was eventually recognised as the Indian pattern.

India's Olympic gold in 1928 had meant for them a surge in the popularity of the game. As recruitment increased and hockey began to be regarded as India's national game, the business of local stick manufacturers prospered. Most were now being made of mulberry and since it was difficult to replicate the English shape there were a number of failures. Rather than waste them the toe ends were reduced, rounded off and sold cheaply to the poorer children for a few annas.

As happens with children there were always spare moments - before and after school and during breaks. Those keen on hockey would play around in pick up groups in any free area, however confined, dreaming, maybe, of the day when they would play for their Country. Inevitably, dribbling would predominate and what the viewer slowly realised was that these children were developing remarkable stick skills - the reason being the facility offered by the shortened heads for reverse side play by means of a simple turn of the wrist, as opposed to the unwieldy English stick which required both the right arm and shoulder to move across the body. As adult players watched and pondered, the penny began to drop. One or two asked manufacturers if they would purposely make them a stick with one of these shortened crooks. The Indian stick had arrived.

Conditions during and immediately after the War meant British exports of sticks dried up. The Indians benefitted. Exports of their new model spread rapidly except in Britain where, during the early years, converts were confined mainly to those who had spent some of their wartime in Asia. The rest were bedevilled by tradition.

Unfortunately for progress, the different shapes required different rules. The Rules chapter and the main narrative explain the problems and the time it took to make adjustments.

In succeeding years there were changes towards even smaller crooks. The trend was started because of advantages for indoor hockey and artificial surfaces since in both cases the ball effectively remains on the ground as opposed to the occasional bounce on grass. So, provided the size of the crook did not much exceed the diameter of the ball, a stop to the left of the body could be achieved simply by laying the stick horizontally along the pitch. An added bonus was a quicker reverse side turn with the wrists.

In terms of refinements there have been regular changes to shaft sleeves and bindings which by reducing the 'give' increases the hitting power. There have also been aluminium shafts and shafts with bends in them based on the theory that since the transmission of hitting power from wrists to the point of ball impact is in a straighter line it is therefore more efficient.

The hitting power of the modern design has now reached its safety peak. Future changes hopefully in the mind of the F.I.H. Equipment Committee will be how not to overpeak.

CHAPTER 10

THE HOCKEY BALL

Even the hockey ball has a history. The story can be told briefly in three parts - first anything hittable, then whatever type of ball cricketers might decide to use; today, only the most meticulously tested.

Early missiles

It is probably best to ignore the period prior to say 1800 when any movable object hit by a stick was cited as the missile for whatever game the writer was concerned with. Let us also agree to omit the absurd but regularly quoted inefficient, so called, use of brass balls in 1272 B.C. when they were said to have been hurled - ergo hurley, ergo an ancient form of hockey - by one group of Irish to kill another. (The exact year, for what in those days must have been a trivial event, seems, somehow and for some reason, to have been carried down for more than three millenia although there is nothing to confirm the then existence of brass foundries!).

The best starting point when sticks were one handed pieces of wood is a repetition of the Cassells quote of 1867:- "The hockey ball must be one fitted to receive hard and frequent blows. Anything in the nature of a cricket ball is found to be ill adapted for this peculiar game, as the leather soon bursts, through the effects of the knocks received from all kinds of rugged pointed sticks. A large bung, strongly tied and quilted over with string, is a favourite and an inexpensive ball for the purpose; and the best of all is, perhaps, a solid india-rubber one, or the larger part of a thick india-rubber bottle, firmly closed at the end from which the neck has been cut". (A search has been conducted for a number of years without success for an old india rubber bottle. If anyone discovers one it would make a welcome addition to the H.A. museum).

Balls of various materials covered with string had been commonplace but, once the potential of rubber was realised in the early 1800's, that became the most popular especially at schools such as Mill Hill, St Eliot's of Blackheath, Marlborough and Rossall. The problem was the bounce. Experiments with compounds and vulcanisation had only just started and when rubber received a hard hit on open ground it would bounce away out of control - even out of sight. Hence Blackheath's resort to the shape of a cube. Perversely, with age the bounce would diminish and the rubber harden, although elasticity could be restored for shortening periods by boiling the ball in water.

The cricket ball

Then from 1871, in spite of the sting, there was Teddington's adoption of the cricket ball and the modern game. Once spliced sticks appeared, it was this ball which was instrumental in changing hockey from a hit and rush, anything goes exercise, to a more scientific passing game.

To begin with it was just a cricket ball; then by the time the present H.A. had been set up it had become a cricket ball `painted white' with other types being accepted by agreement of the captains. The standard was modified to white leather with a twine and cork interior but still with a freedom for alternatives. A number appeared during the period of the 1930`s depression for balls were a major expense especially if there was no source of throw outs from a cricket club. One cheaper plastic version was known as a `compo' a variation of which even had simulated stitch marks. They were never used for county or international games. They did not have the same feel on the stick, and being unpopular eventually faded from the scene.

The cricket ball itself was not ideal. When brand new on a dry, level, well cut surface the clip of a crisp hit imparted a lovely feeling but it faded all too soon. In rain or simply because of a wet surface, a used ball would lose colour, the leather would swell and the gap at the seams would widen for which reason there arose the custom of having available a box of 6 balls a game. With one exception - see note about Battersby among the miscellaneous comments at the end of the chapter - the suitability of the material, the weight, and the circumference were just accepted. The rules specified the use of a cricket ball, so a cricket ball it had to be.

The most unsatisfactory feature was the stitching for cricketers liked to have more than was strictly necessary for manufacture as an aid to swing with a new ball and for break bowling once it got worn. It was of no significance for hockey except for the player. When the ball flew up into his face he not only got bruised, he was just as likely to get a cut and so need a few stitches of his own. In the days of grass and the English stick it was not too serious. The 'give' in the stick, the often heavy damp grounds and the prevalence of pushing and flicking all limited the average pace of the ball compared with the sometimes frightening speed of today.

At length there was the advent of synthetic surfaces. Falling over often grazed a player's skin so pitches, particularly in hotter climes, were watered both before the game and at half-time. Wet balls, subjected to the impact of modern sticks, would lose colour enough to lessen their clarity on television and with repeated use would swell and wear more quickly.

The change-over

For FIH tournaments the choice of ball was of commercial advantage. In the early 1980's Rene Frank, the F.I.H. President of the day, was reluctant to make any changes and he had had recent occasion to imply to a manufacturer on the F.I.H. list that it could expect leather type balls to be used for the next Olympics. A nice story goes, and it sounds credible, that while chairing a meeting at the end of a long day he nodded off in the warm atmosphere. His committee, in favour of a change, quietly passed a resolution to use a plastic, seamless ball with golf type dimples for their next international tournament.

There may be doubt about the truth of the story. There was none about the success of the experiment. The image on television and its playing advantage were improvements enough for a similar choice to be made for the next tournament, since when plastic has held sway.

Once the breakthrough with tradition occurred, changes abounded with a variety of cork and twine insides backed by a broader rule allowing material of any colour, sewn or seamless, subject always to the standard weight and circumference requirements. The FIH then went further by authorising a new Equipment Committee to prepare a definition of a ball which, in return for the payment of a fee would bear their specific approval. The choice, admittedly, needed to be exclusive but their specification would appear to have gone over the top.

Testing

For example, such a ball has to be tested for weight, dimensions, surface characteristics, centre of gravity, surface friction, durability, water absorption, shape recovery not to mention rebound and hardness at three different degrees of temperature. And these are not superficial exercises. Take the 'Hardness' test made with five balls randomly selected from a manufacturer's batch.

The initial hardness starts with an official rating quoted as 155 plus or minus 30. Each specimen is then placed on a flat horizontal steel plate resting on a concrete base. A steel missile of 5 kg mass with a plain lower surface is allowed to fall 1.1 metres (not a mere 1 metre, mind you) on to the ball. An accelerometer mounted on the missile is used to measure the peak rate of acceleration. This acceleration expressed in gravities is reported as the hardness. The hardness is checked after water absorption and shape retention tests. The maximum change to the mean of the five results at 23 degrees Celsius may not exceed 12% and 25% respectively. (At least that's what it says and one bets you never knew).

Consider next specific gravity. Modern players will, doubtless, know all about it, but a survey among past players revealed that few had realised the significance which its variation from the geometric centre must have had upon their play. The knowledge has since put a quite different accent on their reminiscences in the bar.

105

Ball measuring equipment used at the 1980 Moscow Olympics and marked to that effect. There have been stick rings but no-one had previously thought of having equipment which would ensure the balls used were of the correct circumference i.e. not more than 9 and a quarter inches nor less than 8 and $^{13}/_{16}$ths. The Russians, sensitive of their image at the time, were not going to be caught out. Two specimens were made for the occasion. This one, kindly presented to the Teddington museum, is believed to be the only one now in existence.

Today's test makes quite sure the variation will no longer be a hazard with which a player has to contend. Some may like to have the details. It is not too difficult.

Three mutually perpendicular axes are marked on the ball. The ball is then put in a holder with one of these axes parallel to a balance beam and weighed. The axis is turned round the other way and weighed again. The process is repeated for the other two axes with the six resulting weights denoted as X+, X-. Y+. Y-, Z+, Z-. They are likely to vary, but do not worry. The centres of gravity of each are obtained by means of a straight-forward formula taking into account the mass and permitting a calculation of the average of the errors. To obtain the distance between the geometric and gravity centres one simply applies the formula:-

E (the error) = the square root of (X squared + Y squared + Z squared)

One can understand the need for detailed checks on sticks and artificial surfaces but is so much necessary at this early stage for balls? The majority of games are still played on grass where rebound and surface friction are going to be more affected by the climate and ground than by consistency of manufacture. There are also two types of rebound test. First of the ball itself tested by a drop on steel set in concrete. Then there is another applying to the rebound of an approved ball when an artificial surface is being tested.

Progress cannot be halted, but is it going too far too fast? At this rate a player may one day find himself being tested for weight, durability, centre of gravity, liquid absorption, friction, hardness and shape recovery. With the fun going out of the game at the top, this could happen. The Olympics have already resulted in a highly scientific system of drug testing.

Miscellaneous comments

To the FIH - These are not serious comments - you do a grand job. Indirectly the information may help what is being done to be more fully appreciated.

To the players - Do not worry. Remember that subject to the weight and circumference requirements the FIH allow an extra-ordinary amount of latitude in respect of balls for club games.

Ball testing

There is only one early record of anyone questioning the suitability of a cricket ball for hockey - H. Prevost Battersby, who played for Surbiton and Surrey in the 1890's, an interesting character said to have hunted elk, wolf and bear in sub arctic parts of northern Europe, and who, for the experience, tried living the life of a peasant in one of Tolstoy's provinces during the famine of 1892 and then went off as a volunteer to the South African war.

With the co-operation of a London manufacturer he conducted experiments to see if the ball could be improved. One aim was to try out a larger and lighter ball, which being less destructive might improve the play. He tried endless materials - thread, cork, wool, linoleum, linen, flannel, bamboo root, rubber, skins, gabardine and so on. Every ball satisfied some desired requirement; there was none which satisfied them all and in the end he gave up.

First use of cricket ball

Smith and Robson in their book `Hockey' published in 1899 mistakenly reported that it was East Surrey - they had ceased to exist some 23 years earlier - who introduced the cricket ball to the game.

The facts are that East Surrey were formed in late 1874 by W.B. Richardson who on visiting his brother, a master at Marlborough, was so fascinated by a fifteen a side stick game which was being played with a rubber ball (The school did not adopt the cricket ball until 1876), that he decided to copy it and so founded the East Surrey Club.

On 16th January 1875 Richmond agreed to play them and an account of the game was published in The Field magazine. East Surrey lost but as The Field explained, they were at a disadvantage - not only had they to conform to the Richmond rules, they had to use a different (hard) ball. East Surrey next challenged Blackheath who agreed to a match with them if they played the Blackheath type of game which they did. The account in Smith and Robson's book stated that East Surrey brought along for information a copy of `their' rules (i.e. those they had acquired from Richmond who had drafted them in readiness for the impended setting up of the 1875 Hockey Association - and to the inaugural meeting of which East Surrey had been invited). Such rules, of course, referred to the use of a cricket ball which had already been in use for four years.

A writer without The Field background misconstrued the Blackheath report and gave East Surrey credit for the introduction both of the rules and the ball. Dagg in his book `Hockey in Ireland' copied the Smith and Robson account. Others then followed.

Chapter 11

The origin of artificial grass

Back through the ages games had always been played on natural, normally grass, surfaces. How is it that pitches such as those used for baseball, American football and hockey now consist of artificial grass?

A generally accepted account states that a senior member of the Ford Foundation watching children at play in a New York slum area suddenly realised they had probably never even seen a green field. Knowing friends at Monsanto were experimenting with carpets of synthetic fibres to replace wooden or linoleum covered floors in offices, he asked them if as a one off exercise they could extend the idea and lay an extra large carpet of simulated grass in a school playground, which they did.

That might have been the end of the story had it not been for trouble at the Houston Astrodome built in 1965 as the world`s largest indoor sports facility. A crisis arose when it was found grass would not grow under artificial lighting. Recollecting the school experiment, Houston asked Monsanto if they could repeat the process. They accepted the challenge with success. It became a precedent first for Seattle where the surface of a new open air stadium in a rainy climate would quickly change to a sea of mud, then elsewhere in the U.S.A. and now world wide.

Synthetic Surfaces
The Joker who Revolutionised Hockey

By 1972 the FIH had acquired world control of the game except for the IFWHA whose absorption was only a matter of time. It was short of money. Hockey was not a spectator sport and the pessimists still had a feeling there was a risk of exclusion from future Olympics. Recruitment seemed to be in decline. It might have been a propitious occasion for the setting up of a Committee to review the state of the game and make recommendations about its future.

Had it done so, it is quite certain there would not have been a recommendation, at a then cost of some £500,000 a time, to introduce artificial pitches. Apart from the effect upon tradition after a hundred years of grass, the concept would have been judged financially unrealistic and no Council of the FIH would have dreamed of agreeing to such a proposal. Even if an individual Association or club had had the resources, it would hardly have risked incurring such a cost only to find the pitch competitively unacceptable to the opposition. So, how did it all happen?

There is an excellent report prepared by a member of the FIH Equipment Committee about its evolution. It is wholly factual, omitting the background, and saying baldly, inter alia, 'Thus, when the FIH was presented with the proposal from the organising committee of the 1976 Montreal Olympics to host the Hockey Tournament on synthetic turf, favourable reports enhanced the chances. Rene Frank, the FIH President, then witnessed an exhibition match and on his recommendation the surface was unanimously approved for Montreal.'

The report did not add, as was the intention, `but only for Montreal because of the exceptional circumstances'. The background - understandably omitted - is a fairy story.

It was the whim of a Canadian hockey enthusiast; a bachelor, stockbroker, playboy - you must allow a degree of literary romancing, one Peter Buckland whose Vancouver club, appropriately enough, was called the Jokers.

Buckland had been an international player, hardly of Indian or Dutch calibre, but one nevertheless, and an Olympian to boot, who played at Tokyo in 1964 when Canada for the first time became the American Continental qualifer. The game was his hobby and when the rotation for his Country's Presidential appointment came round to British Columbia, it was he who was chosen with the first co-incidence of many - that his period of office overlapped the Montreal Olympics.

Find a level surface and Buckland would play hockey on it -indoors or outdoors. He had established a festival on the sands in Victoria Island and when the Empire Stadium was built in Vancouver with a synthetic surface for baseball and American football, it was not long before he had persuaded the

PETER BUCKLAND Twenty years on

authorities, when it was free, to let the Jokers try out some hockey on it. The surface, of course, was a joy. He organised more games and being imaginative thought, idly, what fun it would be if they could have such a surface for Montreal.

His Presidential responsibilities took him to Montreal to check on the arrangements from the Canadian Association angle and he mentioned the thought to his opposite number at McGill University. I wish you could, was the response, we are desperately keen to get such a surface for our football, but the cost is quite out of the question. If only you could persuade the Canadian Olympic Committee it is necessary to have such a surface for hockey that would do the trick because all Olympic costs are being funded by them and once it was installed we could take it over.

With the backing of John McBride and Victor Warren, Joker colleagues who for practical, locational reasons were also serving as C.F.H.A. officials for the Presidential term, plus the passive but willing support of McGill, they then connived at -or at least went in for - a fair amount of exaggeration.

Superficially, they had a plausible case - something along these lines. Winters in Montreal are severe; the area is covered in snow for most of the period so, with a consequent poverty of grass quality, the FIH had to face up to a real possibility of the tournament being spoiled for, not only would the hard wear

Council members at the Christchurch meeting were presented with samples of the Monsanto turf shaped in the form of a maple leaf. This museum specimen must be one of the very few still in existence.

of continuous games ruin the surface, an inclement spell of weather could make it unplayable. In any event, by the time it came to the final the poor condition of the pitch would not do justice to the occasion and that would not be good for the image of hockey at a time when its inclusion in future Olympiads was still not guaranteed. The prudent decision would be to play safe and use a synthetic surface. (The practical, obvious alternative, apparently not mentioned but always adopted in the past, was simply to have other pitches in reserve.)

Rene Frank was not a President with a closed mind. He watched an exhibition game and was ready to be convinced. He asked Buckland and his colleagues to attend a tournament at Christchurch in New Zealand to put their case to the

Council who would be meeting there. Monsanto, sensing a business opportunity, also sent representatives and what was more in those non-sponsorship days offered to the fairly cash strapped FIH a subsidy to meet the cost of publishing a World Hockey periodical, a project dear to the heart of Frank.

The gods were at hand. The heavens opened and for a period ruined the pitches. The lesson was noted and as a consequence it was decided to stage a trial tournament in Toronto in October 1975. Incidentally, probably on grounds of cost, neither India nor New Zealand participated.

The trial was ranked a success and in the special circumstances the Council agreed to go ahead. Note the `special circumstances'. There was no record of an intention thereafter to repeat the experiment. Particular conditions had produced a one off problem. It had been faced and duly solved.

As a spectacle Montreal turned out well, but to the world of hockey, the result -Gold to New Zealand - was a surprise. To bronze medal Pakistan and medalless India it was a disaster. At the three previous Olympics New Zealand had been 14th, 7th and 10th. Pakistan had been 2nd. 1st and 2nd, with India 1st, 3rd and 3rd.

One can only have sympathy for the Indians who were 7th. Their's had always been a game of attractive stick skills. This was something new - a test of power and speed, of hard hitting and fitness for which, because of their absence from the trial tournament, they were quite unprepared. No praise can be spared for the New Zealanders who took their chances and adapted so well. It was said the Indians travelled home separately to avoid demonstrations of displeasure at the airport. It was also rumoured the Manager had his home burned. The fairly justifiable excuse was that this was not a proper hockey tournament - that the conditions were artificial.

The heat died down slowly: but there were repercussions. Give or take an odd inaccurate detail, the pattern went broadly like this.

Prior to Montreal, the Germans, gold medal winners at Munich, had persuaded their Government to help them retain their title by laying down for practice an artificial pitch at Limburg. Having finished a disappointing 5th, they applied for more help and got it. By 1979 they had four pitches with another planned for 1980.

After Montreal, the Dutch, through absorbing circumstances, became the front runners. In spite of protests, the Kampong Club had part of their ground taken over compulsorily for new road building. As compensation, and to allow twice as many matches to be played within the reduced area, the Local Authority suggested they provide them with a synthetic pitch. Since at that time Kampong were a 2nd Division club, the Dutch Federation agreed, deciding that any advantages gained for home league matches had, in the circumstances, to be accepted. Not so for Rotterdam. Their ground was below sea level and suffered from occasional flooding. They had the funds and decided to follow suit. This time the Dutch Federation said no because they were a 1st Division club. Rotterdam took them to Court and won.

Holland is a leading hockey country. Clubs run 50 to 100 teams. Space is at a premium and pitches have to take a lot of wear. With such large memberships it was not all that difficult for the bigger ones to raise the funds, if necessary with long term borrowing. The Rotterdam result opened the doors for these richer clubs. By 1979 five of them had pitches and there were seven more planned for 1980.

The F.I.H. stood back and watched. Although at Montreal they had had no thought of the synthetic surface experiment being repeated, they had not forgotten that the pitches at the last two World Cups - Kuala Lumpur in 1975 and Buenos Aires in 1978 - had been ruined by rain.

The number of major tournaments was increasing. The expenses of hotels and world travel were becoming too heavy a burden for programmes to be cancelled or postponed. The F.I.H. might by then have hoped for the use of artificial pitches but they could certainly not yet impose them when only the richest clubs or occasional Government support could meet the cost.

Moscow were hosts for the 1980 Olympics. There was no compulsion, but what the West could do the Russians were anxious to prove they could do equally well. They decided, to the relief of the FIH, that their tournament should also be played on a synthetic surface.

Over this period the number of countries with artificial pitches had increased to include England with three, and Western Australia, Wales, Spain and Pakistan each with one.

What policy should the FIH adopt? It was a difficult situation for less than 10% of affiliated Associations had pitches with use limited to their top echelons - well under 3% of men players, and less so for women.

Should they award tournaments only to the `Haves'? What about the rules? Should they be reviewed for the benefit of the elite? What about the umpires? Recognised competent operators from countries solely with grass pitches were now sometimes found to be out of their depth at the start of a game and needed both to be fitter and to have time to adjust to the pace and tactics associated with artificial grass.

The potential market

Parallel to these problems was the potential market for a new industry. Synthetic grass offered a clear advantage. The game need no longer be a hostage to the weather.

The level surface made it so much easier for children to play and enjoy the game. It provided consistent conditions for home and away matches and with a pitch being available for 3 matches or more a day, a club had economy of scarce space and less ground wear.

In 1984 the hockey playing population was probably just under 4 million and growth was accelerating. (An estimate of 8 million in the official Olympic Review of 1984 would seem to be too high). Ignoring the constraint of cost, this could have meant a potential demand for 60,000 pitches. At £500,000 a time the market could have approximated to a staggering £30 billion. So how were the manufacturers re-acting? Not very positively. Perhaps they were too realistic. Their early marketing and competitiveness seemed to depend on cosmetic improvements e.g. modifications of the foundations and, to help drainage, replacing the initial practice of a camber with permeable surfaces -important but of little effect on the prime consideration, the initial cost. Once more the gods moved in.

Turn now to sport in general. Growth at the grass roots, a reflection of changing social attitudes and leisure, was fairly modest. It was faster at the top. Easier air travel was producing more tournaments with increased national pride and higher performances, leading to more spectatorship and the earlier stages of wider T.V. coverage, commercialism and sponsorship. All of which meant heavier losses for major outdoor events susceptible to poor weather.

Two sports with successful T.V. images were golf and lawn tennis. Owners of golf courses realising the potential of artificial surfaces asked a manufacturer to see what he could come up with for the greens.

He started by analysing the make up of a typical surface. Fine grass has delicate roots for which reason the soil on the greens needed to contain a substantial proportion of fine sand. This in turn would contribute to the characteristic run of the ball and its 'feel' when it was putted. Sand, therefore, had to be a constituent of any realistic alternative.

The experiment was not considered successful but one lesson learned was that the addition of sand permitted the use of a coarser, tougher and therefore, cheaper synthetic grass. The manufacturers switched their research to tennis court surfaces and a number were installed in Australia. The makers then moved to tennis courts in Holland at which stage the Dutch National Sports Federation commissioned an investigation into the potential for hockey pitches, very much conscious of the advantage of a 40% or more reduction in cost.

The report, though recognising the lesser quality compared with non-sand versions, was favourable. The Dutch approved them. It meant a substantial widening of the affordable market and between 1982 and 1987 some 160 of these pitches were installed. Clubs in other countries followed suit and at last it allowed the FIH to be confident of the direction in which hockey surfaces and therefore the characteristics of play - as well as policy - would travel.

The changeover was a shot in the arm for a game with a modest image. There are now well over two thousand artificial pitches in use and the number increases annually. It is invariably the surface used today for major leagues and tournaments; and when used by lower adult teams and children they happily string together four or five passes - a skill unknown in the days of heavy, uneven grass surfaces. That such an unpremeditated, unplanned, apparently financially impossible change should have occurred is indeed a fairy story. Three cheers for the machinations of Peter Buckland and his Jokers.

Footnote

The scarcity of pitches for the next five or six years meant there were few opportunities for women to use them, certainly not enough to study the effect upon their style of play. That did not occur until the 1988 Olympics.

An image of a typical top woman hockey player would have been a many capped English physical education teacher at centre half. Strong, experienced, well built, there she would stand, four square, controlling the middle of the field, stretching left or right to intercept clearances or to rob a dribbling member of the opposition, before looking up briefly to assess the situation and send a penetrating pass back to one of her forwards. The Dutch, Germans and Australians were similar. At Seoul in 1988 their Asian counterparts could not have been more different.

The South Korean side, for example, were chosen from a young squad who had first qualified as athletes capable of minimum sprinting standards. Their skills could not compare with those of the West, who by comparison looked on average half a stone overweight, but when in possession of the ball, their speed allowed them to give their opponents a wide berth without sacrificing positional advantage. The message registered and these days the Dutch, British, Germans etc. are all leaner and play the faster, fitter game which artificial surfaces demand.

The new type of pitch has provided another bonus - increased recruitment. In the days of grass, too many girls with wrists weaker than those of boys, having spent their time at compulsory games hacking away in groups on heavy winter surfaces, would leave school sighing with relief at being able at last to throw away their sticks. Now - and more and more at the junior training sessions of local clubs - they find their play enjoyable and open, and with the ball easier to hit as they wiggle and wriggle like old stagers.

Natural history
A sad experience with a happy ending

The story begins with an admission of hockey's inadvertent cruelty to elongated invertebrates. Happily, maternal wisdom came to the rescue and there is no longer anything to worry about.

When artificial pitches were first laid, no-one thought of isolating them from the contingent areas of grass or the impossibility of explaining to worms what was happening.

As a consequence the poor (literally) little perishers finding before them a beautiful new sward, entered the territory with gay abandon, convinced they had discovered something not only new but free from such molluscular competitors as slugs.

But, as they crawled further and further into the virgin land, they found not only was there nothing to eat, there was no way of burrowing. By that stage they had travelled too far, lost their bearings and were unable to get back. The wind blew, the sun shone, they began to starve and eventually died.

Fearing an outcry from Greenpeace, the hockey fraternity kept quiet except for the Teddington museum curators who, in spite of a degree of opposition, felt they should at least record the phenomenom. Hesitating about the method they decided eventually to preserve one of the deceased in a test tube, sparing no expense by using only the purest of pure alcohol and displaying it, unostentatiously, with a deferential explanation.

Fortunately it was realised by the end of the season that the bodies were no longer appearing. With it becoming evident that mother worms were now warning their offspring of the deadly danger, it was decided the exhibit could be removed.

Chapter 12

Apocryphal tales of hockey's antiquity

Although nothing to do with modern hockey here for those who might be interested are some comments about various apocryphal stories of hockey's antiquity. Since such an exercise might be considered tasteless the examples are limited to one or two just for the purposes of illustration. It is also an excuse for showing off the results of some useful research on the Beni Hasan tomb.

When modern hockey started it had no history other than that of its immediate antecedents e.g. hurley, shinty and bandy, mainly because the conditions of earlier life, travel and communication meant that opportunities for recreation were rare and confined mostly to children who, beside romping, throwing stones etc., would have hit loose objects with clubs or sticks.

The opening clause of one of the oldest books, `Hockey', written by Battersby in 1895, is revealing - "If it were of as much advantage to a game as to a woman to be without a past, hockey might claim an enviable position."

There were, in fact, no suggested origins until many years later when two events co-incided - the discovery in the 1920s of a piece of wall said to have been built around B.C.500 by Themistocles and depicting two Greek youths with crooked sticks trying to do something with a round object - maybe seeing how high they could lift it without it being dropped? The other feature was the onset of one or two forty and fifty year anniversaries of English clubs which led writers to reflect upon histories.

Thereupon the growth industry started. It was said the piece of wall was proof that the ancient Greeks played. It was followed by claims that Romans, Byzantines, Chinese and Persians also played. So too had South Americans taught, it was reported in all seriousness according to one writer, by Indians of Asia who had travelled there westwards via Europe before the continent of Atlantis had submerged. Not to be outdone, another writer (both of them had forgotten in the first place that it was the British who had introduced the game to India) agreed, except for the direction of travel. He claimed it was eastwards at a time when the Asian and American continents were supposed to have been joined! Such eras were reminiscent more of the origin of species than the origin of hockey. But again it does n`t matter: it is symbolic of a Shakespearean reflection in The Merchant of Venice -

Tell me, where is fancy bred
Or in the heart or in the head?

The Egyptians had missed out on all this but in the middle 1920s archaeologists found Tukanhamun's tomb. As research continued so did public interest and to such an extent that by the 1930s there occurred what has been described as the "King Tut craze". Interest spread to other excavations and just after the last War someone, brooding on some etchings in the tomb of Beni Hasan which had been discovered around 1900, decided one was evidence of the Egyptians having played hockey, something the latter until then had never known or realised.

There is a wide range of such claims to examine and if a reader wishes to look for further information, it is suggested he does his own research provided he starts with an awareness of two common fallacies. First, if a painter, who is almost certainly not a knowledgeable hockey historian, uses his artistic skill and imagination to produce scenes of events many hundreds of years before his time, the detail is unlikely to be factual. Secondly, that the bully is of relatively modern origin.

A frequently quoted example comes from what is referred to as the Decretals of Gregory 1X, a 14th century papal decree determining points of canon law and written by an Italian scribe.

Many years later the document found its way to Smithfield in London where an English artist - there is no information about his ever having watched or played hockey or of his having visited Italy, an adventurous undertaking in those days - decided to illustrate it as shown in part by the top photograph on the right.

The two elderly gentlemen portrayed are a little past the age of running, and are probably engaged in some agricultural pursuit. There are no goal posts or other players and the ground looks pretty rough, but since they hold sticks of some kind this is regularly quoted as evidence of early hockey in Italy. The link is obscure. Since agriculture was an important part of everyday life there could, conceivably, have been some connection with Gregorian Decretals. But hockey! What does the reader think?

The second example quoted as early evidence of hockey is taken from a 14th century Queen Mary Psalter reproduced in Hockey News in February 1957 by kind permission of the British Museum. The caption reads "Abel and Cain tend their beasts. With crooks and balls they play together at festivals." But Cain was no friend of Abel and with the population at that time not much above single figures festivals must have been rare occurrences. A simpler interpretation suggests Cain is demanding Abel hands over his apple. In any event one wonders about the reliability of 14th century research into forms of recreation during the Genesis era.

The third feature on the following page is a damaged window, one of twelve in Gloucester Cathedral commemorating the victory of the battle of Crecy in 1346. It depicts a man - the head is missing - with a stick and some sort of round object.

The Cathedral Dean categorically disagrees with both, but hockey and golf `historians' contend with each other in claiming it as evidence of their game being played at that time.

119

Can it really be believed that in the fourteenth century officers of the day (They did not then consort with the other ranks) possessed hockey or golf gear which they included in their kit on the off chance of finding suitable pitches or courses for an occasional game or two? That in the event games were played: and they became such a feature that, when it was decided to commemorate the campaign for posterity by means of a cathedral coloured window, it was thought only right and appropriate that these particular events should be included in the design. Again, what is the view of the reader?

There are a number of similar examples but, reluctantly, that has to be the ration except for something more absorbing - a light hearted example of the ease with which wishful thinking can lead to wrong conclusions.

Hockey 4000 Years ago

The etching above, taken from the South wall of tomb number 17 at Beni Hasan in the Nile valley, is claimed as evidence of hockey having been played around 2000 B.C. It was decided to investigate further - and to leave no stone unturned a visit was made to Egypt to study the country's climate, soil and economy. History books and writings, including those of Herodotus, were consulted.

Apart from the immediate valley of the Nile, Egypt in those days was a sparsely, nomadically populated, infertile area; very hot with a predominantly sandy, desert surface hardly conducive to hockey. According to Herodotus all Egypt at this period was a marsh, except for the canton of Thebes, with none of the land below Lake Moeris then showing itself above the surface of the water. He also added that the Nile, when it overflowed, flooded not only the delta, but also tracts of the country on both sides of the river in some places reaching to the extent of two days' journey from its banks - not wholly useless detail because it does suggest it would have been rather difficult to find any suitable pitches either because of the flooding or because, once the water subsided, the valley, enriched in part by the silt, was then intensively cultivated.

A visit today might lead the reader to question such conditions, but it must be remembered that from 1830 onwards they were greatly changed by the construction of a series of dams.

Beni Hasan, some 200 miles south of Cairo on the east bank of the Nile between Asyut and Memphis was a necropolis, a cemetery of 39 rock hewn tombs, not of kings but of officials called `Nomarchs' in charge of Nomes, i.e. administrative provinces existing during the 11th and 12th Dynasties. They lived in modest palaces built on rock and surrounded by a courtyard. It was not a particularly rich or populated area and the normal recreation of the Nomarchs was reported to be fishing and hunting for wild life found in and around the swamps.

Interest lies with the tomb of one named Kheti which contained the above etching. The circular object is about 12 inches in diameter, i.e. larger than a football, while the sticks from the ground would reach to about the knee. (There is no reason to believe the relative sizes are incorrect because it was the practice for Egyptian artists of that day to adopt what was known as a standard rectilineal type of design). One does not know what the ring - or ball - was made of, nor the sticks. If of wood the latter would not have been easy to acquire, especially for a whole team, because the product in that climate was scarce. There seems to be no evidence of its use for housing or tomb construction and there were references to shortages for boat building. In the absence of supplies rafts had, in fact, to be made of tightly lashed dried stalks of papyrus. A certain amount of wood may have been obtained from Lebanon but because of its scarcity most of it would have would have gone to richer areas such as Heliopolis and Memphis.

So what is the etching all about? If you believe it is a ball used for a type of hockey starting with a bully, try to think through what would be involved, for winning something of that size, or getting it to move any distance with the implements being used, would be an inefficient, not to say an impractical, exercise. Since there could be several interpretations, the Secretary of the British Egypt Exploration Society was consulted. The opinion, confirmed as being in keeping with the view of the Head of the Egyptian Section of the British Museum, was studiously non-committal except for a definite "It would be safe to assume they were not playing hockey".

It was said in the opening chapter that these apocryphal claims do no harm and probably add to the romance of hockey's history. So, why does this account go into such detail with what, one must agree, is a destructive analysis? To tell the truth it is to enhance the denouement.

It has been recognised throughout that there is a duty to the reader, and, of course, to world hockey to be thorough and dispassionate - to eschew prejudice. Take for example, the views quoted above by the British Museum. Why should they be regarded as sacrosanct? What do they know of hockey? Being academics they may never even have played the game.

A return to the tomb for a closer examination of the other 400 odd etchings revealed at last among the Eastern section of the South wall what was being looked for - something an imaginative, enthusiastic researcher might claim was clear evidence of hockey.

Here displayed for the first time is a selection of what could be his interpretation of their meanings. If accurate, it would, of course, be a staggering revelation of tournament conditions more advanced even than those used currently by the F.I.H., -note, for example, the sceptres carried by the Technical Delegate and Umpire as symbols of their authority. In the tense competitive conditions of today it is surely a practice which might well be adopted for the modern tournament.

Modestly the suggested discoveries are offered to the world at large although, in view of the depth of research and its enormous cost, you, the readers are earnestly requested to observe their copyright.

Note: Admittedly, there is an absence of sticks. As happens today before a game, it is assumed the umpires, having checked them with their `one fifth of a cubit' rings, would have required them to be deposited in racks either side of the T.D.s table. Regretfully, it is understood, the researcher omitted to look for a specimen table.

HOCKEY SCENES FROM THE BENI HASAN TOMB

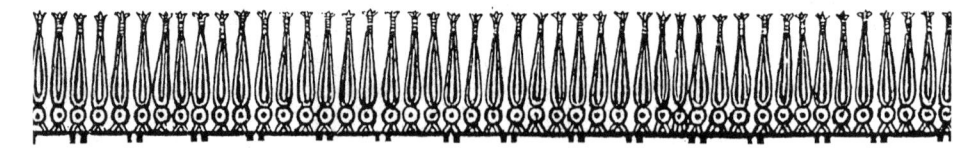

Spectators

Opening ceremony: Releasing the doves

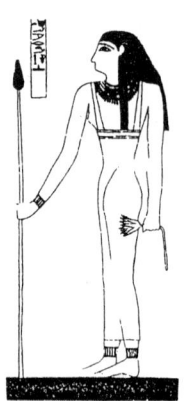

Technical delegate

Umpire

Musical interlude

Removal of gate-crasher

Refreshment for spectators

Programmes - tablets of stone

HOCKEY SCENES FROM THE BENI HASAN TOMB

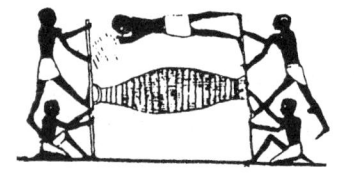

Erecting goalposts

Preparing for half time

Removing an injured player

Subs warming up

The Press, with ink and papyrus

Goalscorer standing on his head with joy

An injury being treated

Sub having footware checked

Ball boys
Even in those days they were inattentive

Appendix 1

Rules of the 1875 Hockey Association

1. The maximum length of the ground shall be 150 yards and the minimum 100 yards; the maximum breadth shall be 80 yards and the minimum 50 yards. The length and breadth shall be marked with flags and the goals shall be upright posts 6 yards apart, with a tape across them 7 feet from the ground.
2. The sticks used shall be curved ones approved by the committee of the association. The ball shall be an ordinary sized cricket ball.
3. The game shall be commenced and renewed by a bully in the centre of the ground. Goals shall be changed at half time only.
4. When the ball shall be hit behind the goal-line by the attacking side, it shall be brought out straight 15 yards and started again by a bully; but if hit behind by one of the side whose goal-line it is, a player of the opposite side shall hit it from within one yard of the nearest corner flag post and no player shall be allowed within 20 yards of the ball until hit out.
5. When a ball is in touch, a player of the opposite side to that which hit it out shall roll it out from the point on the boundary line where it left the ground, in a direction at right angles with the boundary line at least 10 yards, and it shall not be in play until it has touched the ground, and the player rolling it shall not play it until it has been played by another player, every player being then behind the ball.
6. When a player hits the ball any one of the same side who at the moment of hitting is nearer to the opponent's goal-line is out of play, and may not touch the ball himself nor in any way whatsoever prevent any other player from doing so, until the ball has been played, unless there are at least three of his opponents nearer their own goal-line; but no player is out of play when the ball is hit from the goal-line.
7. The ball may be stopped, but not carried or knocked on by any part of the body. No player shall raise his stick above his shoulder. The ball shall be played from right to left, and no left or back-handed play, charging, tripping,collaring, kicking or shinning shall be allowed.
8. To obtain a goal a player must hit the ball between the posts and under the tape.
9. No goal shall be allowed if the ball be hit from a distance of more than 15 yards from the nearest goal posts.
10. In all cases of a bully every player shall be behind the ball.
11. On the infringement of any of the above rules the ball shall be brought back and a bully shall take place.
12. The ordinary number of players shall be 11 a side.

Appendix 2

End of Bully

The bully lasted over 80 years during which period it became the most recognised feature of the game. Its abolition is described separately because the background helps confirm the circumstances of its introduction.

The Indian stick had been in partial use in the U.K. for some ten years. Its greater manoeuvrability, referred to as a licence to cheat, was spoiling the bully which had frequently to be retaken. The players and a majority of the national Associations began to agitate for the ritual to be replaced, but the attitude of the Rules Board, traditional and under British control, was one of caution.

In 1954 the Technical Committee of the F.I.H. made a formal recommendation to the Board that a change be made. The Board, still hesitant, deferred doing so until 1957 and then only after adding a proviso that for the first two years it should be regarded as experimental. In 1959 the bully was officially abolished and the hit out restored.

The Rules Board members would not have known why Teddington had introduced the bully (See Chap 1), but, in explanation of their hesitation in cancelling it, they arranged for an official F.I.H. Bulletin to be issued. The parallel of the thinking with that of the Teddington attitude which, in reverse, had brought about the bully, is significant. Here is the appropriate extract:-

" (The Board) has realised that ..... difficulties may arise affecting other Rules and also that the abolition of the 25 yards bully may give rise to very hard hitting for the purpose of gaining ground from the resulting free hits. (The pitches, remember, were still of grass) .

Very hard hitting was noticeable during the Olympic Games at Melbourne and if continued, could reduce hockey to a slogging match which would spoil a game in which skill should be paramount. The Board has all these points in mind ...".

Note 1: The end of the bully brought about an uncovenanted improvement.

In those fairly casual days, when the umpire blew for a bully, the rules required all the defending side to go back behind the 25 yard line. The forwards would only saunter back for it was a tedious process which had existed far too long. Its abandonment certainly produced a welcome opening up of play.

Note 2. Because it was a strange ritual, the bully became a popularly recognised characteristic of the game: and since a painting or a picture showing two individuals contending with sticks for a ball could, with wishful thinking, be interpreted as such, there arose the mythical claim of antiquity referred to in the opening pages of the book. This more detailed explanation may help clarify the background.

Appendix 3

I.O.C. decisions about the inclusion of team games (Chap 4)

1896, 1900, 1904 and 1912 - no hockey

1920. I.O.C. recommend the exclusion of all team sports except football `which is a democratic game with teams not playing solely for nationalistic motives'. In the event Congress included football in a limited optional list.

1921. A decision was made to exclude hockey from the 1924 Games because the sport had no International Federation. (Football then became the only accepted team sport).

1924. The F.I.H. having been set up and given I.O.C. recognition, hockey was granted re-admission with effect from 1928 in the `Facultif' class i.e. subject always to acceptance by the host country.

1928. The I.O.C. decided to exclude football from the 1932 Games because the players were not wholly amateur. It meant hockey was the only team sport in the programme.

1930. Hockey's inclusion as a Facultatif sport was reviewed and confirmed.

1932. The I.O.C. turn down an F.I.H. application for the inclusion of women.

1935. F.I.F.A. having satisfied the I.O.C. about the amateur status of their players, it was agreed to re-instate football.

1937. Confirmation of the inclusion of hockey in the 1940 Olympics - nullified, of course, by the War. (General eligibility was reviewed postwar and confirmed.)

1947. An F.I.H. request for the inclusion of women's hockey again refused.

1952. A resolution that, henceforth, all team games be excluded was lost - not on judgements of merit, but (a) because it was considered there would be too much of an outcry from the increasingly influential General Assembly of International Sports Federations and (b) because the consequential loss of gate money in respect of football could not be afforded.

1954. (a) Hockey`s participation reduced from sixteen sides to twelve (b) An F.I.H. application for the game to be transferred to the `Obligatory' class refused.

1956. A general warning about the adverse impact of team games, i.e. that too much accent upon national competitiveness was engendering a chauvinism harmful to the Olympic spirit.

1960. A study group was set up to consider the inclusion of women's hockey.

1965. Discussions with F.I.F.A. about the elimination of football because it was a professional as well as an amateur game. Splitting the management of the two sectors was regarded as not wholly satisfactory. An agreement to continue was based on the fact that the sport was played by millions of amateurs and was very popular. However, it was on account of these discussions that British soccer decided finally to withdraw.

1974. The inclusion of women's hockey for 1976 was refused pending a further review of the joint FIH/IFWHA background. It resulted in the admission of 6 teams for 1980 followed by 8 for 1984.

Appendix 4

The introduction of hockey to India

Hockey was introduced to India via the Armed Forces. As the Empire developed, ex-patriots working for such organisations as the Police, Indian Railways, the Indian Civil Service etc. joined in to form their own teams or set up separate clubs, the first of which was the Calcutta Club in 1885 with F.C.Jackson of Teddington being one of the initiators. Pitches were readily available because apart from the various Army Stations, several well appointed residential centres had been built by the British often with married quarters. The grounds were beautifully kept and the lawns watered, if necessary, every day. It led to the setting up of a Bengal championship - the Beighton Trophy - as far as records show in 1895. It is the earliest known competition apart from the Irish Senior and Junior Cups of 1893 and 1894, although the Irish women also claim 1895 as the starting year of their Cup.

Other tournaments followed including the Aga Khan tournament in Bombay around 1896. To start with they were confined to commissioned officers and according to Charles Newham, who held the initial records, the contests reflected the social conditions of the day with the accompaniment of dinner parties, receptions, dances, regimental tents and bands.

The game next spread first to the other ranks and then to native players who, although at that time using the English stick, began rapidly to exhibit unusual sharpness and skills, one theory being that these developed because, instead of having well tended grass pitches, they had to play a faster type of game on hard baked surfaces where a player could only progress if he had top ball control.

(The introduction of artificial surfaces lends support to the theory, for once Europeans, Australians and New Zealanders played on such pitches and adapted to the conditions, they began to close the performance gap. As a consequence neither India nor Pakistan reached the Montreal finals while in the 1986 World Cup they came a disappointing 11th and 12th. Happily, they have since come back to the top but no longer as the undisputed leaders.)

In November 1925 Associations such as those of Western India, Sind, Gwalior, Punjab and Delhi combined to form the Indian Hockey Federation and in 1926 a representative Indian Army side toured Australia and New Zealand. Its success led in turn to the selection of a full Indian side in 1928 and their gold medal visit to Amsterdam.

Appendix 5

A world need for Synthetic Surfaces
(Extract from a 1987 report to the FIH)- see page 79

A long term view

It would be statesmanlike if hockey's governing body could have the time to raise its sights and contribute in a modest way to world social problems.

A recent World Bank Development Report gives statistics and projections of population growth. The detail for the major cities of three industrial countries is as follows.

	Latest census	Projected for 2000
New York	16 million	22 million
Tokyo	12 million	26 million
London	7 million	13 million

The population growth will cause many headaches - and of space in particular for Tokyo. The prime causes of growth are improved infant mortality at one end of the scale and increased longevity at the other. Hockey in making its modest contribution to health and recreation could extend its facilities for children and veterans with the day long use of more synthetic surfaces. Fortunately, these cities are rich enough to be able to provide such resources if only they have the foresight to anticipate the need - which the F.I.H. should stimulate. There were just five cities with populations exceeding five million among the industrialised countries in 1975. By the year 2000 there are likely to be 12.

The real problems belong to the developing and undeveloped countries. Here, all F.I.H. members, are population figures for nine of their cities.

	Latest census	Projected for 2000
Mexico	12 million	32 million
San Paulo	8 million	26 million
Calcutta	7 million	20 million
Rio de Janeiro	5 million	19 million
Bombay	6 million	19 million
Seoul	8 million	19 million
Cairo	6 million	16 million
Karachi	3 million	16 million
Buenos Aires	9 million	14 million

Statistics in the Development Bank report show how the major part of the increase in the world's population from 4.16 billion in 1975 to a projected 6 billion in the year 2000 will be concentrated in the developing countries with the number of cities having a population exceeding 5 million rising from one to forty. How much greater, therefore, is going to be their need for recreational facilities and what a boon it would be to have a number of non-stop playing facilities in the form of synthetic turf. For so many countries financial pressures make the prospects of grants remote; but help from the F.I.H. with illustrations such as these could, perhaps, just turn the scale.

Note:

A comment in April 1996 stated the projections were proving to be substantial underestimates because of a growing tendency for inhabitants of agricultural areas to move into the towns.

Appendix 6

Rugby and the Olympics

Rugby, reportedly, is pressing for inclusion in the Olympic Games and, in particular, for Sydney in 2000. With hockey and football included, how has it missed out?

Following the token game in Paris in 1900 and with the Rugby Union refusing to be involved, rugby of a sort was played in 1908, 1920 and 1924. The first consisted of a Cornwall County side playing and losing to some touring Australian Wallabies while in 1920 at Antwerp a scratch American team beat France.

During 1924 Baron Latour`s requirement that each Olympic sport had to have an International Federation then came into force but in the case of rugby was not followed up.

British refusal to set up a Federation for hockey had not stopped the French from taking the initiative. So why in identical circumstances did they not do so for rugby when the game in their country was at least twenty times more popular? They could confidently have called for support from Roumania, Germany and Italy, perhaps a medal winning U.S.A. and Australia whose touring side had won in 1908. That would have made six applicants compared with hockey`s seven from Europe but it would have meant a wider geographic spread.

The most likely reason could have been the unfortunate chain of events at the 1924 Olympic final between France and the U.S.A. both of whom had beaten the only other participant, a weak Roumanian team.

The French, quoted as 5-1 favourites, had won two games earlier in the season against sides from the Home Countries, while the Americans, drawn mostly from Stanford University, were not regular rugby players but American type footballers. They were not recognised officially by their U.S. Olympic Committee and had had to pay their own travelling expenses.

On their arrival at Boulogne, the validity of their passports was questioned by the French Customs who tried to send them back to England. After a great deal of hassle, delay and the intervention of the U.S. Consul, they were eventually allowed to proceed, arriving in Paris long after midnight with no-one to meet them and nowhere to stay.

When the two sides met for the final (Convincingly won 17-3 by the U.S.) an unfortunate head-on collision resulted in a French player, who happened to be the star of their side, having to leave the field. No substitutes were allowed in those days and, to make matters worse, another French player twisted his knee in the second half and also had to retire.

From the first departure a large, unruly, non rugby playing section of the 20,000 odd spectators, who were said to have laid substantial bets upon a

French win, went in for sustained booing of the Americans which continued, to the dismay of the French officials and team, during the presentation ceremony and the playing of the U.S. national anthem.

The game itself was sporting and the hospitality generous but, in the light of the Olympic ethics which Coubertin had stressed so strongly, the combination of circumstances must have left the French too embarrassed to initiate a campaign for participation.

It was a sad experience which, had it happened at a less critical time, would probably soon have been forgotten.

Appendix 7

Conversion on the road to the Alchemists

In 1973 Wales went to Prague to play Czechoslovakia.

At around 10.45 on the evening before the match, the three accompanying selectors, having dined well, were wending their way back to the hotel and passed a tavern from which emerged familiar sounds of laughter. On inspection they found it was the Welsh team and their manager, Roger Self. Hardly good preparation for the morrow's game. Having told them to get back to the hotel, the selectors met to decide what to do and agreed that Graham Dadds, the Chairman, should reprimand the manager.

The morning programme involved a visit to the famous street of the Alchemists with their ambitions of finding a way to turn dross into gold. On the way Dadds, a forthright character, did not mix his words. Self was hardly backwards and instead of a five minute conversation the argument lasted over an hour. In the event they only got as far as the beginning of the street but Self became converted. The following year, with him still in charge, Wales with the poorest side but the most committed players, won the Home Countries championship beating all three rivals. The hallmark of selection, which the manager never forgot, was character. That particular team, for example, included at centre half no Oxbridge blue, but a fairly crude ex-soccer player, edges smoothed, but one so determined he would never rest or give up.

While Wales continued to prosper, the G.B. side were in the middle of a disastrous run - twelfth at the Tokyo Olympics, twelfth at Mexico and a modest sixth at Munich. They did not even qualify for Montreal.

The English had a nominee for a new manager. The Welsh demurred and suggested Self: but one or two of the H.A., having experienced some of his outspoken views, would not agree. The Welsh persevered, wooed the Scots and eventually on a two to one vote got their way.

The rest is history. G.B. had failed once more to qualify, this time for the Los Angeles Olympics in 1984. When one country withdrew, they were called in as the reserve side and won the bronze. Then, four years later, the gold at Seoul again not with the most skilful side but the one with the best team spirit - and, of course, a Manager with a bit of alchemy.